TIPPING THE SCALE

Tipping the Scale

The Book That Changed Everything You Know About Investing in Cannabis

Michael Brubeck

LIONCREST
PUBLISHING

TIPPING THE SCALE

The Book That Changed Everything You
Know About Investing in Cannabis

ISBN   978-1-61961-656-1   *Paperback*

978-1-61961-657-8   *Ebook*

This book is dedicated to my father and all
of the great teachers in my life.

Contents

Foreword

I first met Michael Brubeck nearly a decade ago, when he walked into my law office seeking legal advice on running his medical cannabis business. Navigating the complex web of regulations, and operating within the boundaries of California State law at that time was like trying to study particle physics with a textbook missing half its pages. Not only did he come across as smart, ambitious, and sincere, but he was also meticulous about not crossing any lines in an industry so surrounded by ambiguity.

In a sense, he was trying to be the first man on the moon in the emerging legal cannabis realm—a pioneer, making his own footsteps rather than following those of others. He wanted to push the industry forward in ways few others had the foresight, vision, or courage to imagine. He's still the same way.

Over the years, my relationship with Michael has evolved into a great friendship, and I am delighted to be writing the foreword of this book. He and I have been pushing the boulder uphill in the effort to expand cannabis legalization for a while now—Michael from the business side, and me from the legal one.

I graduated with a BA from Harvard University and a JD from the University of Texas years ago with a young man's idealistic passion, and a social mission to change the world. My first stop was Washington, DC, where I began my law career with the Federal Election Commission—a US government agency dedicated to regulating campaign finance. I toiled to keep politicians honest for five years before getting fed up and moving to the Bay Area of California, where I set roots and practiced election and business law. On the side, I performed pro bono work for patients trying to gain access to medical cannabis. In those efforts, I found my calling.

Today, my practice entirely involves medical cannabis. I'm older and somewhat wiser but with the same passion and world-changing social mission. To me, there is no greater failure in American policy than drug prohibition, especially with marijuana. This beneficial herb has been used to great benefit throughout human history, and for the US government to make its possession and sale subject to severe criminal sanctions is the absolute height of folly.

Denying its access and punishing those who need it defies the basic concept of human dignity.

Medical cannabis is simply the tip of the spear in the slow, grinding battle toward reversing the injustice of across-the-board cannabis prohibition. More than eighty years of anti-marijuana propaganda has taken its toll on public perceptions, and those of us involved in the fight still face powerful interests allied against us. Yet, in the face of this opposition, we have celebrated many important victories, starting in 1996 when California voters passed Proposition 215. This initiative made the state the first in the country to legalize medical cannabis for patients. I personally am fighting the good fight on the streets, in the ballot box, and in the courthouse, as I have filed the only two cannabis-related cases to be argued in front of the US Supreme Court.

Michael's work on the entrepreneurial side is just as important—and impactful. Few people I know have the courage he does to constantly be pushing open doors in the cannabis realm. He is, and always has been, a leader. In turn, the whole industry has benefited from his work, not to mention the patients who use cannabis.

Michael's latest venture, Centuria Foods, takes his work to an impressively large scale by expanding internationally, to yield results in cannabis production never seen before. Centuria has the potential for great success not only on the balance sheet, but in producing quality products and services that help humankind.

The cannabis industry is not for the timid, as Michael and I know too well. It involves risk, and Centuria is certainly not immune. People who want to succeed in this field need backbone. They must be willing to risk failure. I could go on, but this is Michael's book, and I don't want to give away too much of what he eloquently covers. So, let me conclude by sounding a call to action to all of you readers. Right now, we're in the nascent, pivotal stage of the legitimate industry. It can still move in any number of directions. If we continue to follow the correct path, we can improve human rights and truly change the world. However, it will require a mass effort.

I hope the information here will give you greater understanding of the work ahead of us to change the world, and if you're an entrepreneur, it will encourage you to join the effort—whether your motivations are guided by principle, profit, or both. For those of you already involved in the cannabis industry, I hope these pages offer a better insight into how to succeed in your work and help us win the fight. For those of you who simply want to gain a better understanding of how and why prohibition will end, and what will take its place, I hope Michael's book provides clarity and inspiration.

—ROBERT RAICH, ATTORNEY AT LAW

Introduction

———

To understand the present and future of the cannabis industry, it helps to understand yogurt. Yes, yogurt. In 2005, Hamdi Ulukaya bought a shuttered Kraft Foods factory in New York with an $800,000 loan funded largely by the Small Business Administration. He hired master yogurt makers from overseas and spent two years perfecting a recipe and the right, efficient manufacturing methods. In 2007, he and his new company, Chobani, were producing a yogurt that was thicker, higher in protein, and less sugar-filled than the typical offerings from Dannon and Yoplait found in the dairy sections of supermarkets.

He didn't stop with quality. Hamdi sold each cup of his yogurt for $1.50—about half the price of Greek yogurts sold in health food stores, and almost as low as the popular American yogurts found in grocery stores.

The price was calculated to allow Ulukaya to break even, once he sold 20,000 cases. At this volume (according to his article in the *Harvard Business Review*), Hamdi would have the revenue to rapidly scale his business once Greek yogurt's popularity grew. Now, ten years later, Chobani is a Fortune 500 company that has cornered nearly 20 percent of the $6 billion US yogurt market.

How did he do it? He ignored the standard product offerings and production methods in his industry, and he created a breakthrough business model.

Chobani is just one example of a company stepping outside of industry norms, thinking creatively to seize massive market share in an industry ripe for change. Apple's iTunes, which generates $16 billion in annual revenue, decimated its competition. So did Starbucks, which brings in $21 billion annually. Can you even remember where the #1 place to get coffee was before a little company from Seattle took over the country—and the world?

This is where cannabis enters the picture. It's another industry ripe for breakthroughs, and it's a hell of a lot larger than yogurt.

We're not talking about your dad's lumpy joint in the back of a van forty years ago. Far from it. I'm referring to a scientifically, industrially produced agricultural crop that is going to revolutionize every industry it touches. Cannabis isn't just on the verge of a massive image overhaul—it's already happening. Attitudes and assumptions about cannabis are shifting around us in real time, and have been for a while.

Even so, farming and manufacturing methods haven't changed in decades among most cannabis producers. For that reason, the global cannabis industry (both legal and black market) generates $200 billion a year in revenue, yet not a single company owns more than a 1 percent market share.

Think about that for a moment. Did you start to get a little excited when you read it? If you didn't, this may not be the book for you. That's the kind of opportunity that changes your life and puts you on the cover of *Time*, if you can get there fast enough.

There is no behemoth in the cannabis industry positioned to fight off competitors, leaving the entire industry open to a company with a breakthrough business model to seize a massive slice of the North American market, which will easily top $1 trillion in shareholder value in the next decade. Because of that vacuum, the scales are tipping toward massive consolidation. Within five years, no more than a dozen well-financed companies will corner 80 percent of the market.

It's going to happen.

How do I know this certainty? My company, Centuria Natural Foods, operates, at scale, a breakthrough business model for the industry. It has rapidly, when measured by gross tonnage, become the largest legal manufacturer of cannabis in North America. No other company is positioned to dominate the US market the way we are. As prohibition barriers fall, we are like Chobani without any Dannon or Yoplait for competition. To put this into perspective, in the past year or so, Centuria has manufactured and processed more biomass than the combined flower output of every US state that reports tonnage production, as well as all legal cannabis in Canada put together. In addition, we operate our primary extraction facility at less than 10 percent capacity.

THE GAME-CHANGING MOMENT

In 2009, America's cannabis business emerged from the shadows. The United States Justice Department issued a directive to federal prosecutors on February 27 of that year, telling them to stop seeking convictions on growers, distributors, and buyers of medical marijuana who adhere to state laws. The order became famously known as the

Ogden Memo, named after the deputy attorney general who signed it, David W. Ogden.

After the memo's release, newly inaugurated President Barack Obama's spokesman, Robert Gibbs, told the press the document simply reiterated "administration policies" from the day the president took the oath of office. Asked if this stance would lead to other states legalizing cannabis, Gibbs said, "I'm not going to get into what the states should do."

Afterward, the *New York Times* quoted an American Civil Liberties Union representative who called the decision "an enormous step in the right direction, and, no doubt, a great relief to the thousands of Americans who benefit from the medical use of marijuana."

In truth, the Ogden Memo was more than just a step; it was a game-changing moment. Those in the cannabis industry who carefully abided by state laws got a massive break. The environment of fear had been lifted, and a giant roadblock to a free market was removed. They no longer had to worry about federal officers decked out with automatic weapons and body armor breaking down their door like they were terrorists.

We knew this time would come—eventually. The pendulum

of history was bound to swing in favor of cannabis, it was just a question of when. Few people outside of my colleagues and I, carefully watching the political winds, realized it would happen so decisively or soon.

President Obama campaigned on the platform of change, and what could have been more indicative of change? The two huge topical issues of that time were marijuana regulations and gay rights. He turned the tables on both, as he said he would. It didn't hurt that popular opinion across the country was on his side.

In the states, the Ogden Memo took a tremendous amount of pressure off governors and legislators. With the White House's stance saying, "This is the direction the federal government is going, so if you have an overwhelmingly high level of support in your state for medical cannabis, then that's okay," they were free to listen to their constituents.

Without the threat of Big Brother looking over their shoulders, state-level lawmakers held more meaningful, civil, and—frankly—open discussions on ending cannabis prohibition. They debated more freely on how to craft legislation that would enable sick patients to benefit from medicinal cannabis without somehow being labeled as soft on crime. Drug policy became more sensible, and these ripple effects caused an earthquake of activity among industry retailers.

Within twenty-four hours, the market flooded with opportunists.

These unprepared early adopters had no concept of how the business worked. Most of them seemed to come from the real estate industry—from bankers to mortgage brokers to realtors—who had once been rolling in cash during the housing bubble and looked for a quick buck to put them back on top. They saw marijuana as the next bubble, especially in California, Washington, and Colorado, because these states had enacted laws to allow patients to grow cannabis collectively and for retail marijuana dispensaries to exist.

Most of the other fourteen states to legalize medical marijuana were too ambiguous on how patients could pool their resources and how businesses could—and couldn't—set up shop. State enforcement was inconsistent and difficult to understand, so retailers were raided by both the state and the federal governments, even when the business owners thought they were conscientiously operating within the boundaries of the law.

Michigan was a prime example. There were no regulations outlawing retail dispensaries, so many retail businesses set up shop. There were no rules on how they could operate, either, so there was an oppressively high rate of police raids—with little rhyme or reason as to where and when the raids would take place. For instance, one week in May 2015, law enforcement officials raided eight dispensaries in northern Michigan, while 250 others operated openly and untouched across the rest of the state. In late 2016, all dispensaries in Kent County in western Michigan were raided. The rationale behind why they, specifically, were targeted, despite believing they operated under the letter of the law, is unclear. A month later, police teams stormed every dispensary in Grand Rapids.

The ensuing legal hassles made doing business in Michigan prohibitive. Dispensary owners therefore focused on California, Washington, and Colorado, where the number of cannabis dispensaries grew exponentially in the years after the Ogden Memo. Fortunately, the legislature and governor in Michigan adopted new, clearer licensing rules for the medical cannabis industry, wiping away many of the previous legal hassles.

They followed in the footsteps of California legislators, who have had incentive to establish clear-cut cannabis guidelines. The Golden State was the epicenter for innovation in cannabis cultivation after the Ogden Memo. Marijuana was (and still is) California's largest cash crop—though most of the product went straight to the black market, unregulated and untaxed.

Growers in Southern California and the Emerald Triangle in the north cultivated immensely popular varietals perfected by expert growers. California couldn't ignore the need for enforceable rules the other states were, or a Wild West mentality would have erupted in the newly burgeoning industry. Still, even in the Golden State, some ambiguities remained.

After the Ogden Memo, the retail cannabis industry became a frenzy. It had all the indications of retail values becoming a bubble themselves, like some of us predicted in 2005 in real estate (a major factor in my personal pivot into cannabis in the first place), so I shifted my focus. Everybody and their brother was jumping into cannabis retail—but who was making moves into cannabis supply?

I looked at it this way: Crowds of entrepreneurs shelled out money to buy the cannabis equivalent of gas stations, but no one thought about becoming an oil and gas company to supply the crude. The supply chain, at that time, consisted only of small growers, just as it does today. The challenges for growing cannabis on a large scale seemed insurmountable to many investors and entrepreneurs—from state regulations, to limited supplies of water, real estate, harvesting technology, capital, and plain-old knowhow.

The people who thought that problem didn't have an answer were, and still are, misguided.

In 2012, voters in Colorado and Washington overwhelmingly approved ballot measures legalizing the sale of recreational cannabis in both states. The following year, the Justice Department issued another decree, called the Cole Memo, named after the deputy attorney general serving at that time, James Cole. This one told states that federal law enforcement officials wouldn't interfere with state recreational cannabis laws if the market was tightly regulated, sales to minors was prohibited, and marijuana wasn't diverted across borders to other states.

With the Cole Memo, more antiquated barriers against cannabis were lifted, and the movement to end prohibition in states across the country gained meaningful momentum. Within five years, a total of nine states, from Alaska to Maine, legalized recreational marijuana, and today many others consider doing the same.

My decision to focus on the manufacturing end of the business posed many challenges as the regulatory environment shifted, but in turn, it has created an unprecedented opportunity. The doors have opened to a newly forming industry that already boasts a vibrant consumer base. Economists believe its revenues have already exceeded $200 billion in the world.

These are exciting times. At the forefront of the rising

cannabis revolution is my company—Centuria Natural Foods. (There's a reason they let me write a book about it.)

Centuria has developed proprietary technologies and strategies that enable us to produce cannabinoids, the active molecules in cannabis, at a vastly lower price and higher volume than any other company. We also have mastered scale, tipping at 262 tons for the previous twelve months.

To put that into perspective, all 2,600 producers in Colorado sold a mere 143 tons of flower in the same time period. Washington State in 2015 only produced 8.9 tons.

I wrote this book to serve as a roadmap to understanding the legal cannabis industry—how it operates, its history, the directions it has taken and will take, and how it is radically and dynamically changing overnight. Being intimately tied to this marketplace, I have an interest in cultivating a better understanding of cannabis as an evolving industry, and promoting intelligent investment in it.

This book also talks about how my company, Centuria, has uniquely positioned itself to take advantage of evolving cannabis legalization across the country. Centuria's breakthrough business model is a flesh-and-blood proof of concept, operating in the marketplace today. We're not just talking the talk or theorizing. We talk about the real-time data from the trailing twelve to twenty-four months of real-time operations of an existing company. A company that operates at a scale greater than the entire flower output of the 3,500-plus companies in Washington, Colorado, and Canada combined.

As for cottage industry growers reading these pages, I am sounding an urgent and sincere message to you: Your future survival will depend on radically changing your business model. For reasons I explain later, you need to collectivize your efforts, or your business will be swept aside by the tidal wave of mass production barreling toward you from the horizon. There are common-sense solutions at your disposal, if you're willing to recognize and follow them, and I hope you do. Our industry is stronger for your contributions and presence, and, personally, I root for you to thrive. I hope you consider my advice.

One final, important note: The cannabis space is advancing and evolving so quickly, there is a strong chance that weeks, days, or even hours after the first edition of this book is published, some seismic and exciting, game-changing new development will occur—for Centuria, or the industry, or both. The cause could be market-based, technological, or due to added government deregulation, or a million other reasons. What will remain the same, though, are the basic guiding philosophies for cannabis production and consumer psychology I outline in this book. They are timeless, regardless of the speed of change.

I have learned a great deal during my years in the business, and I'm happy to share my insights, successes, and failures. The industry has come a long way in the short time since the Ogden Memo. Hopefully, this book will make you as excited about its future as I am, because it's already exciting, and it's only getting more attractive by the day.

State	Stability	Opportunity	Estimated 2017 Marijuana Sales *
Alaska	B	A	$25 million – $50 million
Arizona	B	C	$325 million – $375 million
Arkansas	C	A	None—sales are not expected to begin until early 2018
California	D	A+	$1.3 billion – $1.6 billion
Colorado	B	B –	$1.5 billion – $1.6 billion
Connecticut	A	C+	$30 million – $35 million
Delaware	B	C	$4 million – $6 million
Florida	C	B –	$20 million – $40 million
Hawaii	C+	B	$15 million – $30 million (in first full 12 months after dispensaries open)
Illinois	B	B	$75 million – $85 million
Louisiana	D	C	None—sales are not expected to begin until early 2018
Maine	B	A	$30 million – $40 million
Maryland	C	A	$20 million – $40 million (in first full 12 months after dispensaries open)
Massachusetts	C	A	$50 million – $75 million
Michigan	D	A	$100 million – $150 million
Minnesota	B	C	$10 million – $20 million
Montana	C	C+	$15 million – $25 million
Nevada	B	A	$120 million – $205 million
New Hampshire	B	C	$6 million – $12 million
New Jersey	B+	C	$20 million – $25 million
New Mexico	A	B	$55 million – $75 million
New York	B+	B	$20 million – $40 million
North Dakota	B	C	None—sales are not expected until mid-2018
Ohio	C	C	None—sales are not expected to begin until the second half of 2018
Oregon	B –	B	$510 million – $580 million
Pennsylvania	C	B+	None—sales are not expected to begin until mid-2018
Rhode Island	B	B	$25 million – $30 million
Vermont	B	C+	$5 million – $7 million
Washington DC	B+	C+	$8 million – $12 million
Washington state	B+	B	$1 billion – $1.1 billion

* This table includes states where marijuana sales are already underway or are expected to begin in 2017; totals include both rec and medical in states where applicable. Sales projections for medical or recreational markets where sales are expected to begin in 2018 or later can be found at the end of this chapter.

ONE

A Creative Approach

My life looks nothing like a Cheech and Chong movie. There are no blazed up, late-night quests for White Castle, no ridiculous stoner hijinks. I don't use marijuana medicinally or recreationally (though I profoundly support the personal rights and liberties of those who do).

I am passionate about my work, because I am an entrepreneur with a creative streak—and no business today requires more ingenuity, grit, tenacity, or *balls* than legal cannabis commerce, since its creation over a decade ago.

I have probably achieved more firsts in the cannabis industry than anyone else. We all know there are no real resumes in the entrepreneur business, just track records of success and in this industry, our corresponding rap sheets. So, here is mine:

In the early 2000s, during the time of the George W. Bush administration, I spearheaded more than a dozen turnarounds at legal medical cannabis dispensaries, resulting in over $100 million in revenue for the owners of companies who were previously on the verge of bankruptcy or battling stagnant growth.

I succeeded with the first eight-figure capital raise in the space with a cannabis investment fund in 2007.

By 2010, I was the first entrepreneur to acquire an industrial-scale cultivation-only permit in North America, for my company Delta Allied Growers.

Currently, with Centuria, I run the first manufacturing company to break one hundred tons of goods manufactured in a year.

The market is so new, the demand for the product so immense, and the antiquated laws restricting it are evaporating so quickly that traditional business practices don't yet apply. Think social media marketing, or credit default swaps. The playbook for this industry is still being written, and I have the good fortune of being among its innovators—though standing at the leading edge has meant a setback or two along the way.

Not that I would change any of it.

When I was a kid growing up in California, I never imagined I would go into the legal cannabis business. I am the youngest of four children in a family who always found a way to blend creativity with industry—two traits that are a must in my current profession. My mother was a minister, and my father was a successful restaurateur. Through the daily coaching of my father, I learned multi-unit operations systems at an early age, which lent the ideal skill set for an all-cash industry with a propensity for theft, from both internal leakage and armed robbery.

My first foray in business was as a paperboy in San Luis Obispo on California's Pacific coast at age eleven. I delivered the local *Telegram Tribune* to houses around my neighborhood and within months, was operating the largest route in town. I became a mini mogul in the eyes of my buddies, acquiring other neighboring routes, mapping out the most efficient delivery plan, and creating an effective system of collecting and receiving payments. Even at age eleven, optimizing inefficient systems was a natural attraction.

After being identified as especially gifted in math, I enrolled in a college close to home at age fifteeen, then eventually transferred to the University of Hawaii, where I dropped out to work in mortgage banking.

In the summer of 2000, when I was nineteen years old and still in college, I started a painting company with a close friend. He had worked for a big student house painting outfit the previous year and had reached out to me with the idea to put together our own venture. He had a nuts-and-bolts knowledge of how we could make the operation work, and I knew I could easily handle the financials and learn California's regulatory structures. It was an ideal pairing.

The catch was the contractor's license. Before our business could be granted one, state laws required at least one officer in our company to possess four or more years of experience. After some research, we found a painter who fit the description, made him a director, and my buddy and I obtained a California contractor's license as teenagers with an aggregate experience of four months between the two of us.

At the time, I lived with my father, and he coached me every morning for roughly an hour on how to run the business and manage my short-, medium-, and long-term goals. We discussed risk mitigation strategies, operational strategies, *everything.* Our talks became a daily ritual, and a form of bonding time that lasted nearly a decade as I transitioned to different ventures and business fields.

My father started a few dozen successful restaurants in his career and became a leading consultant to just about every major food chain and franchise in the US before his retirement. I have always admired his business acumen.

Within six months, the painting company took off. We booked tens of thousands of dollars in business a week and had hired more than a dozen employees. Through connections made by my partner's dad, we received a glowing recommendation from the biggest general contractor in Sacramento and used it to land several commercial and new construction contracts.

We had started solely with residential work before expanding into commercial projects where the real money could be made. Less than six months into the venture, we landed a massive new construction contract. It would have required us to expand more rapidly than our comfort level (and lack of expertise) allowed, so we sold the company to a larger painting contractor who could handle the work.

My experience with the painting company taught me a great deal about the business world and partnerships—and how challenging it can be for two wildly idealistic but well-meaning nineteen year olds to run a successful company. It gave me a taste for running my own business. It also taught me of the importance of being able to scale a business rapidly if demand rose off the charts. Most importantly, though, I realized I wanted to be an entrepreneur.

I reached my next professional milestone in the summer of 2003, at age twenty-three, when I took a job in a large mortgage bank. After a short time, I grew frustrated with the glaring inefficiencies and waste in the company's business model, and their murky ethical practices, so I started my own firm. By age twenty-four, I found myself operating a mortgage bank with a federal banking charter, employing fifty people.

The numbers side of the mortgage business appealed to me greatly, but I found the work monotonous and lacking the environment to innovate. Around that same time, the California legislature passed Senate Bill 420, legalizing medical cannabis collectivization in the state, which opened the door for retail operations to legally exist for the first time in the history of our nation, even if at only the state level.

Dispensaries sprouted and a whole new industry arose with billions of dollars in potential revenues, as if it was pulled out of thin air. I always thought the prohibition of cannabis was illogical, and I could see a revolution emerging on the horizon, like a massive, transformative wave. With Senate Bill 420, it was time to paddle out and catch that wave. I had my chance to become a pioneer.

The problem in the business then, as it is now, is few legal cannabis producers think big. Everything is small-scale. Even Los Sueños Farms in Colorado, the largest licensed nursery in the US, is only thirty-six acres—producing roughly ten tons annually.

Part of the reason is a lack of resources, along with a lack of understanding of the future market. Another reason is the unfounded fear of the federal government reversing its deference to states on law enforcement. Nobody wants to go to jail for being a drug dealer, but that's not a logical outcome if you're paying attention.

Outdated mindsets will ultimately become catastrophic to anyone who doesn't break free from them. So, what's the modern mindset? How can you change your thinking?

Typical "large scale" cannabis producers work with one- to four-acre nurseries, employ eighty to 150 people per acre, and use the same growing methods that have existed for decades. Their cost of infrastructure investment is between $8 million and $40 million an acre, and the cost of goods ranges between $1.50 to $4.00 a gram. With my company, Centuria, we can deploy a complete vertical solution for only $28,000 per acre and produce a similar competitive product made in Canada for 4.4 cents a gram.

You read those numbers correctly: $0.044 a gram, versus $1.50–$3.00 using the typical method. Let that sink in a moment. Remember that feeling from when we talked about Chobani? Centuria Natural Foods is one of the only companies capable of drastically undercutting the global cannabis market.

This efficiency of scale is what is going to revolutionize the market in the coming years, as the barriers of interstate and international commerce are inevitably lifted. That is where the potential for breakthrough business approaches lie. Regardless of which administration is in the White House, there will be federal regulatory change that allows for interstate commerce of cannabis products, and will enable licensed nurseries outside the country to export into the US. The continued trend in overwhelming popular support will demand it.

Before you get too excited—this race will only be won by the swift. The top 1 percent of legal cannabis producers who can scale rapidly when the moment arrives will gain a massive advantage in the market.

For most growers, doubling or tripling their capacity in a year would be extremely difficult—not only due to lack of funds and resources, but because their methods are so outdated and inefficient. Increasing by tenfold would end them.

Let me give you another example of the importance of rapid scalability. In April 2012, the new photo sharing app Instagram enjoyed so much success it generated 30 million new users through its app for iPhones and iPads in a matter of months. So, the company released its first version for Android devices, and within twelve hours received 1 million more downloads. Imagine if it could not have handled the skyrocketing demand. Given the fickle nature of social media consumers, it would have vanished from people's consciousness faster than you can say, "Myspace." In all, it is estimated that only 10 percent of companies can achieve profitable growth over the course of ten years, per the *Harvard Business Review*.

With the model that Centuria follows, growth can be expanded by a factor of one hundred in a year, and we can seize that market share instantly, while maintaining a profit throughout. As proof of concept, Centuria has increased its tonnage throughput each season by a factor of ten in 2015 and again in 2016. In 2017, we are expected to slow to roughly 400 percent over the previous year.

Here is an analogy to the current common production methods in legalized cannabis: Imagine the textile industry during the seventeenth century. Let's say a hypothetical factory owner during this time employed fifty people working at looms that were the most advanced in the world, cranking out yards and yards of fabric per hour. One day, an investor approaches the owner and said, "I'll give you unlimited resources to create more product."

What would the owner from that time do? He would probably buy 1,000 more state-of-the-art looms and hire thousands more workers. He would also need much more factory space to house all the employees and equipment, so he would spend more money either leasing or purchasing the necessary space. Efficiency would not improve, however, only volume of his output. Most cannabis producers today use the same kind of approach.

A typical grower employs eighty to 135 people an acre, doing all the work by hand—from propagation to harvesting. If an owner wants to expand to one hundred acres, he will hire 13,500 people to work the area. This model does not work if you try to expand quickly without sacrificing quality or the ability to meet demands. With Centuria's modernized, scientifically based and mechanized model, we fast-forward centuries ahead, employing less than two people per acre.

Our biggest challenge for growing by a factor of one hundred would be to make sure John Deere can supply enough tractors and combines for us.

Even if investors in a traditional grower see profits now, once all barriers are lifted, this house of cards will tumble, and fast. If they focus on the retail side, which most investors do, their potential returns are limited at best. I'm often asked why I don't return to the retail game. I have no desire to wade back into that bog. Besides, even the best retailer in the world is dependent on a wholesale supplier.

I realize if I can out-innovate other traditional manufacturers by having a cost of goods that's one-fiftieth of theirs, I have a much greater competitive edge than operating one hundred retail stores that, no matter how efficiently they are run, are still at the mercy of a wholesale supplier. Besides, if I wanted to grab a 30 percent market share from the point-of-purchase side, I would need to open 1,000 stores. On the other hand, as a supplier, I can have two nursery sites, each covering 20,000 square acres, and I have accomplished my goal. It is a far simpler model than retail.

To use the example from a couple pages ago, it makes far more fiscal sense to be an oil company than a gas station operator—especially if all competing oil companies operate within a cottage industry model, suffering from lack of vision, resources, and technology to boost production by any meaningful measurement.

Most importantly, I believe there is a simple set of rules all successful startups must follow to scale and thrive.

1. Create the right product. It sounds simple, but it's not. Startup owners need to be passionate about what they're selling, and not simply motivated by finding a random concept they think will make them the most money. They need to love what they do and want to provide the best possible product. Think about Bill Gates at Microsoft, Phil Knight at Nike, or Steve Jobs at Apple. Each of these men shared a deep belief in what they sold consumers. The product must also have a high ceiling for potential sales. You can't create a product and make people want it. You need to find a product people will want—even if they don't quite know it yet—and make it.

2. Surround yourself with smart, ambitious, creative, courageous, and competitive people. Breakthrough business models aren't the creations of the weak of heart. Your team members must be comfortable enough with themselves to be unafraid to fail or propose ideas that might seem completely out of left field. They need to have the fire in the belly that makes them want to crush the competition and outshine their co-workers,

even as they strive to row in the same direction to reach the company's objectives.

3. Build a killer—but sensible—business model. Investors should be able to look at your plans and say, "Wow, why didn't anyone think of that before?" The methods Chobani and Starbucks employed to expand and succeed seemed incredibly groundbreaking at the time, but when you look at them now, they make perfect sense.

4. Show that your model works. You can't just tell investors how you plan to scale, and still deliver a quality, high-value product when the time and demand arrives. You need to apply those methods already, to prove how easy, seamless, and profitable ramping up production will be.

5. Automation is king. The key to undercutting competitors is to deliver goods at a substantially lower price. Simple enough, right? The smartest way to achieve this end is to cut the cost of manpower to an absolute minimum through breakthrough equipment, technology, and strategies, or by using conventional tools and methods in a groundbreaking way.

6. Always innovate. To be successful long term, your company must be aggressive in improving every facet of its operations, all the time. Larry Bird used to show up at the gym before any of his teammates in the morning, when he was in his prime. He did it, he said, because he was afraid "somebody, somewhere was practicing more

than me." You must always look over your shoulder for someone trying to out-innovate you and ask yourself, "How can we do this better?" Never be satisfied with the status quo.

7. Work smarter, not harder. If another, smaller company has created a killer technology or product that would fit with your company and make it more successful, acquire it. If they're not selling, find a way to partner with them. There's no need to waste the time, effort, and money trying to emulate what someone else is already doing well.

8. Look to the future. Have a clear-eyed vision on where your company will be tomorrow, next month, next year, and ten years from now. Consider the changing variables of the market, and consumer tastes. Create a brand image that will be as relevant to consumers today as it will be to their kids twenty years from now (but know that price will always beat brand identity in the eyes of the cannabis consumer). It's often said Nike is a marketing company that makes shoes. If you see the "swoosh" on a sneaker or a piece of performance apparel, you know what you will get, and who the product is meant for. That identity never changes.

These rules make sense, don't they? They are nothing you wouldn't find in a first-semester Business 101 lecture. Yet, often times, the so-called genius's startups become so obsessed with creating a model they think, on paper, will look irresistible to potential investors, they ignore the absolute basics. Centuria meticulously follows these simple but essential rules while, as I'll show throughout this book, all our competitors fail miserably in meeting even two or three of them. As a result, they are bound to fail. Meanwhile, Centuria will continue to grow, gaining a bigger and bigger share of the cannabis market every year, in a way no other company can reproduce. What we're doing is not rocket science—though it does involve a heavy dose of plant science.

Wholesale Cultivation Overview:
Typical Revenue, Expenses & Startup Costs By Cultivation Type

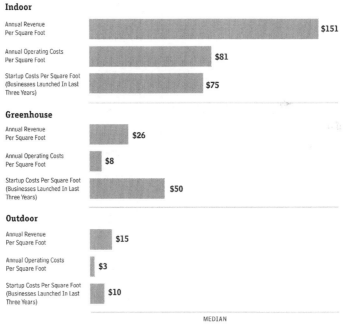

Indoor

Annual Revenue Per Square Foot — $151

Annual Operating Costs Per Square Foot — $81

Startup Costs Per Square Foot (Businesses Launched In Last Three Years) — $75

Greenhouse

Annual Revenue Per Square Foot — $26

Annual Operating Costs Per Square Foot — $8

Startup Costs Per Square Foot (Businesses Launched In Last Three Years) — $50

Outdoor

Annual Revenue Per Square Foot — $15

Annual Operating Costs Per Square Foot — $3

Startup Costs Per Square Foot (Businesses Launched In Last Three Years) — $10

MEDIAN

TWO

An Industry in Flux

I like to think the creative streak that runs through my family has always given me an advantage in business—from my paper route, to the painting company, to today. The legal cannabis industry, given its byzantine—and often undefined—regulations and parameters, requires out-of-the-box thinking to generate solutions. Success in this field takes creativity to understand how the law is applied and how to work inside its margins without crossing any lines.

Creativity is something my parents cultivated in my siblings and me at a young age. I took classical piano lessons when I was two years old—against my wishes, of course. I hated the practice and repetition, but music and the arts, and exercising the right side of the brain, were a priority in my family. When your Uncle Dave is known for something as iconic as jazz number *Take Five*, you take the damn piano lessons whether you like them or not.

When my father decided to open his first restaurant in the late 1960s, Uncle Dave cut him a check for $30,000, no questions asked. Dave Brubeck died in 2012, but he created a legacy that continues through every generation of our family.

Walking into a cannabis dispensary in California for the first time felt like walking into a different universe. It was 2005, and one year earlier the state legislature enacted Senate Bill 420, enabling medical marijuana to be sold legally to qualifying patients. I entered the store in West Hollywood out of curiosity, and there, displayed in front of me, were twenty-five different varietals of cannabis. *There's no way this could be legal!* However, it was.

Still in the investment business at the time, and completely fascinated, I formed a million questions in my head. I asked the owner: "Where does the product come from?" He told me the dispensary worked with 600 to 800 "patient cultivators," which was the title given to permitted growers at that time. Under the state law, only people given permission by a physician could legally possess a set number of plants. They could sell a small amount of excess volume to a medical dispensary to cover their time and materials.

I thought: *600 to 800 patient cultivators. That's got to be the worst idea I've heard today! If these retail stores could work with one producer instead of 800, the prices would be better and the quality more consistent. This is where I want to be in five years.* We're now past a decade.

This dispensary covered only 1,500 square feet of floor space—about the size of an average GNC store—with seven employees handling what must have been a line of twenty customers at that moment. I exhaustively researched the retail medical cannabis industry, including prices, customer base, sales volume, regulations, overhead, everything. The more I learned, the more shocked I was over just how upside down the business model was.

Most of the people who opened dispensaries back then were hobbyist potheads who were satisfied with marginal leakage and taking home a decent salary each month. They weren't concerned with efficiencies. They lived a good life, why change? Why grow?

That sort of thinking drives me crazy.

Any time I step into the front door of a business—any

business—I'm analyzing and assessing how they operate. My motivations are different. On the surface alone, there seemed like so many common-sense ways to shave 10 percent off costs at a typical dispensary here, and 20 percent there. The opportunities in this new industry seemed unlimited and untapped.

I couldn't pivot from mortgage banking to medical cannabis fast enough. I had been living in Sacramento at the time, and packed my stuff to move to the epicenter of the industry at the time: Los Angeles.

Like a true apprentice, I started on the ground floor to learn the medical dispensary business, working first as an assistant manager, then trying out different roles until I was entrusted with running most of the daily operations. From there, I bounced from one dispensary to another, each time charged with improving the business model. At one store, I increased revenue by 500 percent in ninety days. At another, I turned their $165,000 in debt into a cash surplus in less than four months by quadrupling their revenue.

It was clear I had a developed a system that worked. The model was simple: stop theft; be fair to the patient.

Setting up sustainable systems for medical cannabis sellers was not enough for me, though. Maybe it was the business training I got during those long conversations over the years with my father, but my mind quickly jumped to the next step in the evolution of dispensaries: aggressive growth.

Looking back, I probably thought a little too aggressively at times. I was in my twenties, and I put myself in uncomfortable financial places on occasion with my new ventures in the legal cannabis field. However, it was that challenge of maximizing success within a completely new frontier that drove me and was lacking in the rest of the industry.

Before I turned thirty years old and the Ogden Memo was released, I had operated, managed, and turned around the fortunes of fourteen dispensaries—a larger number than anyone else in the business at that time. Still, from the moment I first became involved in the retail business, I knew exactly where I needed to transition: manufacturing. *Control the supply side.* After all, no one else was doing it.

The vision was crystal clear, and it finally became reality in 2016 with Centuria Natural Foods when we passed the one hundred-ton milestone. Today, my focus is aimed at potential aggressive growth, because I realize it's the only way my company or any other in the production end will thrive and survive.

In February 2000, during the height of the dot com craze, a website selling pet food, appropriately named pets.com, went public. Its stock started at $11 a share and rose as high as $14. The company's mascot, a dog sock puppet, even appeared on a million-dollar Super Bowl ad and became arguably the most recognized advertising pitch man this side of Ronald McDonald. Pets.com was the darling of the Internet world. Until, it wasn't. In November of that year, (268 days after going public, to be exact) it went belly-up—liquidating its assets and laying off all employees. More than $300 million in venture capital went poof with it. There are many reasons behind its failure, but the biggest—by far—was this: when it scaled to meet demand, its business model simply became unprofitable. They acquired too much overhead. To be competitive against brick-and-mortar retailers in the dog-eat-dog pet world at that time, they were selling and shipping products at nearly 30 percent below cost, and their burn rate wasn't sustainable.

What does the cannabis industry have to do with sock puppets selling Kibbles 'n Bits? Well, in the next three to five years, 90 percent of cannabis investors are going to lose all their money in the industry. All of it. If you are an investor reading this book, you must make sure you have a mechanism in place that enables you to recoup your principle in the end of 2020. If you do not, you will be hung out to dry. When interstate commerce is inevitably allowed, and the last federal barriers on cannabis prohibition tumble, change will not happen slowly, it will take place over the course of a few of months. All of those companies with fundamentally flawed business models will make pets.com's death look slow and agonizing by comparison.

I know, because I've also watched it happen on a smaller scale in the cannabis business—from the medical side. I've gone into regional markets where I've opened a dispensary and tweaked the purchasing model to acquire cannabis as affordably as possible, then I shaved my margins to undercut my competitors by 25 percent. Thus, many competitors typically lost about 80 percent of their client base within ninety to 120 days.

To apply this lesson to the current market: If a product in Colorado is being sold for $250 per ounce, and I sell something of identical quality for $40 per ounce, the makers of the $250 product will be out of business within three months. Centuria can already profitably sell cannabis at a far lower cost at retail than all other manufacturers can produce it. Until this point in the relatively young history of the industry, prices have remained stable because of the regulatory structures in place creating artificial scarcity. As prohibition falls, the rules of the free market will reign.

How am I confident that the federal government will continue its forward path toward legalization? Simple math, and demographics. Of course, there are no guarantees in life, but all trends continue to surge in a positive direction. Approval ratings for ending the country's cannabis prohibition have risen to 60 percent, an all-time high. That's only seven points behind America's approval rating for baseball. Baseball! Cannabis is one of the rare public policy issues that enjoys support from cities to farmlands and industrial towns, across the political spectrum.

Most encouraging is the fact that younger generations are much more sensible about drug policy than older Americans who were raised in the "Reefer Madness" era of being told that marijuana was the work of the devil. As the years pass, you will see the public approval ratings rise to 65 percent, then 70 percent and higher. Even if politicians are personally against lifting prohibition, they will not be able to hold back the public tide of support. They will not have a choice. That is why some anti-cannabis politicians talk a big game about waging a war on marijuana but refuse to roll back any of the progress the industry has made in the past fifteen years.

Once the tide effectively washes past the remaining political barriers in the country, the demand for economically priced, legally produced cannabis will explode. Scalability among manufacturers will be essential to survive. If you're an investor or producer, you should look at what you're doing or trying to do as a company, and ask if your business model can evolve to a size that's a factor of one hundred or a factor of 1,000 greater than what your initial pilot is. If it can't, you then should examine what must change for it to occur. Think about that Chobani yogurt example I mentioned at the beginning of the book. One of the owner's first thoughts when he set up the company was how he could scale his business structurally, logistically, and financially once sales took off. Centuria has mastered highly efficient systems expanding annually on a massive scale. If we grow by one hundred times, or 1,000 times, there are no growing pains.

To capture 10 percent of the US market share in an open marketplace, a cannabis producer using traditional growing methods would need about 7,000 acres of farmable land and produce 7,000 tons of biomass (or 15,400,000 pounds for those using imperial units). Finding that amount of fertile real estate or warehouse space on an instant's notice, once federal prohibitions fall, would be extremely hard—but even if you did acquire it, you would have another problem: propagation. Nearly all producers today use clones carefully hand-transplanted into substrate to take root. Consider that an acre holds anywhere from 1,800 to 4,400 plants, then multiply that times 7,000. The skilled manpower necessary for that amount of propagation is where the system collapses when scaling.

The next step in the process of scalability is in harvesting the plants. We are the only company in North America that uses a combine for the job. I am not afraid to share this information, because we have spent almost a decade developing custom equipment for it to maximize its efficiency with cannabis crops. Once harvested, the plants then need to undergo the drying and curing process within four to six hours, or they will spoil and mold. Our drying and curing facilities are already operating, and poised to scale easily and affordably.

After the plants are dried and cured, you will then need to turn the material into a retail-ready product. We have an extraction facility that, today, can convert 7,000 tons of dried biomass into a retail-ready format over the course of ten months, including edibles, orals, concentrates, e-liquids, and more. Centuria is also developing a flower-based product through a fully mechanized process that takes the production time from seeding to a retail-ready product to under five months.

Each step in this manufacturing process is a massive, expensive, and time-consuming undertaking on a small scale, and because the industry is still in its infancy, most budding producers have not mastered—or even identified—all of them yet. For these companies to create an efficient process that works on a mass scale, they would need another several years of trial and error at best. Not only does Centuria already own the technology to master each of these steps, we are tipping the scale with this level of output.

When investors look at my company's numbers on a spreadsheet, they understand what I am talking about is not theoretical. I am not referring to systems that Centuria would like to build or develop in the future. Instead, we do these things already. If detractors say, "We don't believe you can grow this much at this scale for this cost," we tell them in response that we're already growing cannabis at a nickel a gram and processing twenty tons a day in our downstream facility in 2016. Our systems only continue to improve with time.

When investors see our projections for the levels we can reach in two or three years, we get no pushback. The only resistance—or skepticism—we receive comes from other industry players. The dispensaries see us, after all, as the juggernaut supplier that they have been fearing for a long time, who will dictate retail prices to the marketplace. They will attack us, but we have the historical data and current production levels being achieved to back up our claims.

Later in the book, I will explain in greater detail the strategies, methods, and equipment Centuria uses to gain its competitive advantages. I am not afraid to reveal the blueprints because my organization historically out-innovates our competitors, despite consistently being in a relatively weaker capital position, and continues to do so in every market we engage. A new company would need at least three years to develop, design, and install the equipment we use—from the specialized tractors and combines to the extraction facilities. Then, once everything is up and running, they would need another two years to optimize use of the new equipment. Meanwhile, Centuria will continue capturing bigger and more market share, all while modifying and advancing our technologies and methods, and crowding out competitors along the way.

The moment our nurseries are legally allowed to distribute high-THC products into the United States or Canada from a foreign, legal source, with our products priced at one-tenth of what is on the market, we will thoroughly disrupt the industry. The effects will echo through segments of the market we do not touch, simply because our capabilities and technologies exist.

So, why are there so many examples of incredibly smart people investing a lot of money in doomed-to-fail cannabis ventures? First, they have trapped themselves within the traditional mindset of how a business in this industry works. (See rules three, five, and six for successful startups in the previous chapter, covering innovation, automation, and a killer business model.) These companies lack the creativity, mindset, and courage to seek breakthroughs. They are also not asking the proper questions.

The doomed-to-fail venture that comes quickest to mind is Privateer Holdings, a cannabis-based equity firm backed by Founders Fund. Privateer boasts a great pedigree at the fund manager level, having been created by MBAs from Columbia and Yale, and they were the first to raise $100 million inside the cannabis space, primarily through legendary visionaries Peter Theil, founder of Paypal, and Sean Parker, who co-founded Napster, pioneering the concept of digital music in the twenty-first century, and was the first president of Facebook.

Privateer's crown jewel was a medical cannabis producer called Tilray, based in Canada. The company built a $40 million, 60,000-square-foot facility in British Columbia, with only one acre of canopy. Their burn rate is through the roof, and they employed about 135 people on that single acre of canopy.

Since going to market, they have failed miserably—almost beyond belief. The founders had no cannabis experience prior to launch, and they simply thought the key to success was to say, "Let's take a lot of money to get the most state-of-the-art growing technology and create the most state-of-the-art nursery, and we'll dominate the market!"

Go on Tilray's website, and it will tell you they operate "one of the world's most advanced" production facilities "ensuring that products are manufactured and controlled per stringent standards."

That is all terrific. Yet, you can also easily find pictures of workers there, meticulously watering plants by hand. Their cost of goods produced is no different from that of other manufacturers in Canada's legal marketplace. All the while, no one among them is asking the right questions. They are only thinking, "How do we make money in the cannabis business?" And the simple answer that came to their minds was, "By growing high quality, expensive pot with excessive electricity and labor costs. Because that's the way it's always been done."

However, that is not quite how the business works. To set themselves apart in the marketplace, they should have searched for potential breakthrough models. They should have asked, "How does our business model scale if we want to rapidly grow by a factor of ten?"

As it stands now, can they instantly raise $400 million to grow a ten-acre site? Can they hold some super-effective job fair for cannabis industry experts that would enable them to expand their employee headcount from 135 to 1,350 overnight? The answers are no.

Tilray is unequipped to seize any significant chunks of market share as regulatory barriers continue to tumble in Canada and the US. Thinking even bigger: What if they want to go from 40,000 square feet to 4,000 acres using the same technology? They would have to raise a half-trillion dollars and would require the manpower of a small nation for their labor force—and they would still be making a product at $3 a gram. Tilray has no answer for producers like Centuria, who have developed new technologies and methods to manufacture products of equal quality but at a fraction of the price. Thus, their investors will be among that 90 percent who will wake up one day soon and wonder where all of their investment went.

Before Tilray spent their first dollar, I knew they had failed. Even if everything went as planned, a $40 million an acre technology is just too expensive. Centuria can expand at $28,000 an acre. There's no way they can close that gap. Look at every single large nursery in Colorado and Washington State, and they too are following the same outdated, inefficient model. Instead of taking chances, they keep following the path of dinosaurs.

If you are a cottage industry grower, you're probably nervous about what this future of mass production holds for you (and if you aren't, you should be). Many small-scale growers follow a similar labor-intensive model as Tilray's, but simply on a smaller scale. If a new company enters the market selling cannabis for 20 percent below the current price, the mom-and-pop players won't be able to compete on their own. You will need to collectivize your growing spaces, manpower, equipment, genetic stock, and practically every other facet of your business to survive. The closed-minded walled-in philosophy of the past won't work.

Imagine if, five years from now, an alien invasion hit the earth. Nearly everyone on every continent would no doubt cast aside their differences and come together to stop the looming onslaught. We would pool our resources, brainpower, efforts, and weapons for the common good and survival. This is the type of philosophy the cottage industry growers need to adopt. The invasion is coming, and they can't isolate themselves from it for much longer. Collectivization is the key to lowering costs and improving production for your phenomenal products so you can stay afloat.

INTERNATIONAL MODELS

Internationally, only two countries have so far legalized recreational cannabis sales nationwide: Canada and Uruguay. A handful of others, like Germany and Israel, allow medical dispensaries throughout. Uruguay officially legalized cannabis in 2013, allowing for growing clubs of up to forty-five members to grow marijuana, and individuals who register with the government to keep up to six plants at home. It also stated cannabis could be sold at registered pharmacies at a set price of roughly $1 a gram, to undermine the black market.

Uruguayan pharmacies have been reluctant to get onboard, though, due to excessive federal regulation and fear of retribution from organized crime. Plus, prospective consumers have to register with the government and submit fingerprints before getting permission to buy legal cannabis—a process that, naturally, scares off a lot of people. Additionally, the mandated price makes legal cannabis production financially impossible for most growers using traditional methods.

Canada's legalized recreational cannabis law goes into effect in 2018. Under it, consumers eighteen years and older can buy from licensed retailers, and citizens can grow up to four plants at home. Industrial marijuana cultivation is already legal under strict government regulation. The market price for medical cannabis in the country ranges from $7 to $12 a gram based on the grade of the product. Centuria will bring that number down dramatically to $1 per gram. This is the future of cannabis.

Economists estimate the domestic market in Canada to be about $8 billion and since early 2016, investment in licensed cannabis producers there has shot through the roof. Market capitalization for cannabis companies like Canopy Growth and Aurora Cannabis have jumped roughly 250 to 400 percent in less than a year, already into the billions of dollars. A "green rush" has formed, but again, most of this money will be completely lost. No one is introducing any paradigm shifting innovation the way Centuria is.

In the US, a similar investment explosion is taking off—and for good reason, considering that the potential market is estimated at $40 billion. By comparison, the American poultry and eggs market totals $42 billion; dairy, $35 billion; fruits, tree nuts, and berries, $25 billion, and tobacco, $40 billion. The green rush in our country in the coming years will make the one in Canada look minuscule. Make no mistake, there will be a few winners, though, and this book is for the investor who intends to win—whether or not it is through backing my company.

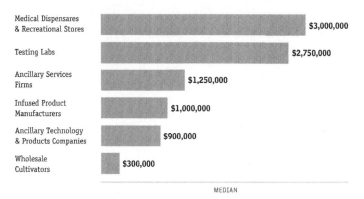

**Typical Amount Of Funding Currently Sought By Cannabis Businesses
That Have Yet To Generate Any Revenue**

Medical Dispensares & Recreational Stores	$3,000,000
Testing Labs	$2,750,000
Ancillary Services Firms	$1,250,000
Infused Product Manufacturers	$1,000,000
Ancillary Technology & Products Companies	$900,000
Wholesale Cultivators	$300,000

MEDIAN

A HISTORY PRIMER

To understand the future of cannabis in America, it is helpful to first understand its past. It is believed the cannabis plant originated in Central Asia—in Mongolia and Siberia, to be precise, and spread from there. Hemp cord was identified in a Taiwanese village dating back 10,000 years, and it is known that cannabis seeds and oil were used in food in China at least 8,000 years ago.

The first recorded reference to cannabis appears in Chinese medical texts around 3000 BC. At that same time, cannabis seed was placed in burial mounds of Chinese nobles, per archaeologists. Over the following centuries, the cannabis plant was taken east to the Korean Peninsula, west through India (who used cannabis as an anesthetic, among other things) and into Persia, and south into North Africa. In India, the sacred book *Zend-Avesta*, written roughly 2,500 years ago, describes hemp's intoxicating qualities.

In North Africa, the Egyptians prescribed cannabis for a wide range of treatments, including glaucoma, and in Europe, the Greeks and Romans wrote of cannabis as a recreational intoxicant and medicinal remedy—and of its use to make hemp fabric. By 100 AD, hemp rope appeared in England, while across the globe hemp paper was invented in China. In the classic Middle Eastern collection of folk stories, *1,001 Nights*, one of the stories is called, "The Tale of the Hashish Eater." Remarkably, cannabis seeds were found in the excavated remains of ancient Viking ships.

In the mid-sixteenth century, the Spanish brought cannabis to the New World, planting it in Chile to harvest its stalks for fabric and fiber. Meanwhile, King Henry VIII made hemp cultivation mandatory in England. All farmers were required to dedicate a quarter acre to cannabis for every sixty they owned. The fibers were intended for rope and other rigging for the country's growing navy. Hemp, after all, is six times stronger than cotton and less resistant to rot and wear and tear. Any farmers caught breaking the law were fined the equivalent of a half-year's wages.

A century later, Jamestown's settlers brought cannabis to

the North American continent, where it soon became an important crop. Mandatory hemp growing laws sprouted in Massachusetts, Connecticut, and other colonies, and hemp was used as legal tender throughout the 1700s. George Washington and Thomas Jefferson grew it on their properties, in fact, and by the 1800s, more than 8,000 cannabis plantations thrived throughout the South and into the Midwest. During that era, more than three-quarters of the world's paper was made from hemp.

Use of cannabis for its medicinal qualities did not arise in America until the mid-nineteenth century, when it became a common ingredient in over-the-counter remedies and pharmaceuticals. It was included in the *Pharmacopeia of the United States*, listed as a treatment for such ailments as tetanus, rabies, dysentery, opiate addiction, leprosy, cholera, typhus, and others. Consumers also used it as an intoxicant. Not until the turn of the twentieth century would a movement arise to prohibit its use—but the motivations had little to do with public health, as I will explain.

THREE

A Checkered Past

I can only imagine the cannabis business a quarter century ago, shortly before medical marijuana was legalized in California. I was fifteen years old then, and more interested in going to the beach and listening to The Beastie Boys than anything else, but I have, of course, heard the tales. Distributors drove long distances across the country, hauling supplies of cannabis in their vehicles. There were no cell phones then, so they kept rolls of quarters in the center console for hitting pay phones—usually to call contacts at other pay phones at prearranged times. Marketing could only be done by word of mouth, and introductions between parties were made through trustworthy mutual friends. Few real names were used, and every transaction meant the potential for serious jail time. Even to this day, my colleagues from that era call me by a nickname they invented over a decade ago.

The environment was closed, organized crime was heavily involved, and the whole scene was dangerous and completely underground. Distributors needed large sums of money to operate, and if people did not pay, matters were resolved far outside the judicial system. A substantial portion of all cannabis sold domestically was grown on the West Coast, from British Columbia to Mexico.

As distributors drove deliveries east from the manufacturing sources, the price would rise incrementally with each mile. Cannabis in Chicago cost significantly more than in Denver. Cannabis in Pittsburgh cost more than in Chicago. The general risk involved—from the mob on one side and law enforcement on the other—inflated prices further. In New York, a pound of cannabis could sell for $12,000. Distributors from California found several creative ways to deliver product. Pilots would be busted carrying 400 to 500 pounds of pot in their small planes. Paranoia among growers led them to create walled-in gardens, and a walled-in mentality that exists today. It was a crazy time, and this system had been in place for decades.

There's one legendary story of a small plane that took off from Mexico in December 1976, carrying 6,000 pounds of marijuana. It was headed for the Pacific Northwest, but crashed near Yosemite Valley deep within the Yosemite National Park, unknown to anyone. A month later, word of the wreckage—and the plane's tail number—filtered back to park rangers, and federal investigators rushed to the scene. They found the plane's remains strewn across a quarter-mile-long path, leading into the shallows of a frozen lake. Some of the plane's bales of pot were frozen into the ice, like insects caught in ancient ember.

Park rangers, armed with chainsaws to cut through the ice, gathered about 2,000 pounds of the cargo, but the conditions were too cold, and the fuselage embedded too deep, to get the rest, so they delayed any further salvage efforts till spring. Word quickly spread, though, of the bounty sitting there for the taking, among the small band of pot loving hardcore rock climbers who basically lived in the park. Soon, they made their way to the lake where the wreckage sat.

A handful of them chopped through the ice and hit pay dirt. Others showed up at the scene by the busload under the noses of park rangers, carrying backpacks with visions of riches filling their heads. They flooded the area like prospectors during the California Gold Rush, armed with pick axes and diving gear, and hauling away water-soaked bales. Suddenly, a handful of climbers became flush with cash, and eventually armed federal agents caught wind of what was happening. They raided the site in April, and the prospectors scattered. The fear of being caught in possession of such large amounts of marijuana sent them far into the woods. Guards were placed at the site, and a full salvage operation by the feds wouldn't take place until that June.

Cannabis was, and still is, classified by the federal government as a Schedule I drug, meaning—in the Drug Enforcement Agency's eyes—it has no medical purpose and has a high potential for abuse. Put plainly, this is a load of horseshit. The designation occurred during the Nixon administration for purely political reasons, and it severely, and needlessly, restricts the ability of scientists or doctors to conduct research studies with it. Other Schedule I drugs include heroin, LSD, and ecstasy. Cocaine is a Schedule II drug, because it can be administered by a doctor for medicinal uses, as are opiates like oxycodone and morphine.

Any scientist or physician will tell you that cannabis does not meet the definition of a Schedule I drug. It is not chemically addictive at all, nor is it dangerous. There has not been a single recorded death from a cannabis overdose in the history of medicine. Ironically enough, the National Institutes of Health, which is a federal agency, holds a patent on the medical benefits of cannabis. The ridiculous notion in the US of cannabis as a hardcore drug, worse than cocaine or morphine, originated more than one hundred years ago and had nothing to do with health and safety.

In the nineteenth century, cannabis was sold at drug stores, mostly in liquid form. Between 80 and 90 percent of medical tonics and tinctures sold over the counter contained at least a small amount of cannabis. The cannabis plant was also grown across the country for its strong hemp fiber. Mexican immigrants largely introduced the concept of smoking pot recreationally to the country in the early twentieth century. During that time, the country suffered by a wave of xenophobia against newcomers from our neighbor to the south.

Anti-immigrant activists, to stoke fear in white citizens and galvanize support for their cause, depicted Mexicans as murderers and rapists deranged by this exotic and supposedly dangerous drug, driven to commit crime. The commonly used word cannabis was replaced with the Spanish name "marihuana," yes, spelled with an "h" at that time, to more closely tie it to non-English speakers and taint opinion against it.

The lead voice in spreading the word of the supposed evils of cannabis was that of newspaper mogul William Randolph Hearst, who stood to gain financially from its prohibition. His company invested heavily in forests and timber mills that supplied wood pulp for paper production. His profits were threatened by the increased use of hemp-based paper, which had become much cheaper to produce, thanks to new harvesting methods. Cannabis is also 800 percent more efficient per acre to grow than timber. His newspapers led the charge in publishing articles demonizing "evil marihuana."

During the Great Depression, as unemployment, poverty, and desperation across the country soared, so did resentment toward Mexicans. In 1930, the US government created the Federal Bureau of Narcotics, which was the precursor of the DEA. Its first chairman was an ambitious former prohibition agent named Harry Anslinger. Prior to his new job, he said cannabis was harmless and the notion that it drove people to violence was an "absurd fallacy."

Upon becoming the country's top drug cop, though, he quickly looked to broaden his power and authority. At the time, only cocaine and heroin were outlawed, so he became a passionate crusader to outlaw all recreational drugs in the country. Suddenly, his views on cannabis changed. It was nothing short of a creation by the devil himself, as Hearst had argued. To sway more Americans to his view, he played to their racism.

"Reefer makes darkies think they're as good as white men," he once said. Another time he announced, "There are 100,000 total marijuana smokers in the US, and most are Negroes, Hispanics, Filipinos and entertainers. Their

Satanic music, jazz, and swing result from marijuana use. This marihuana causes white women to seek sexual relations with Negroes, entertainers and many others."

Marijuana was a threat to America's identity and society, thanks in part to this one man. By the early 1930s, nearly half of the states banned it, and in 1937, Congress passed a law making its possession a crime, based almost entirely on Anslinger's testimony. During the hearings, he quoted a letter from a Colorado newspaper editor that said, "I wish I could show you what a small marihuana cigarette can do to one of our degenerate Spanish-speaking residents." His propaganda war worked, because Americans—including legislators—knew so little about cannabis at the time.

Ironically, during World War II, the US government launched a "Hemp for Victory" drive, giving farmers hemp seeds and granting draft deferments to farmers who grew the plant for use in ropes and other military supplies. In 1944, the New York Academy of Medicine formed a committee requested by New York Mayor Fiorello LaGuardia to study the effects of smoking marijuana among the city's residents. Through its research, it concluded that cannabis was not addictive, nor was it a gateway to morphine, heroin, or cocaine. It was not the determining factor in the committing of crimes, nor commonly used by juveniles, nor did it lead to the deviant behavior alleged by anti-marijuana activists. Anslinger personally led a crusade to undermine the commission's report, and ultimately it fell on deaf ears. Nearly a decade later, in 1956, the federal government set mandatory sentences for possession of marijuana. A first-time offense carried a minimum of two years' imprisonment.

THE SAD BUT TRUE STORY OF *REEFER MADNESS*

Almost every American has heard the name of the anti-marijuana propaganda movie, *Reefer Madness*. It has become a cult classic, alongside *Rocky Horror Picture Show,* because it may just be the worst, least realistic film ever made. People watch it at midnight showings at art houses for the irony. The movie poster calls reefer "The deadly scourge that drags our children into the quagmires of degradation."

It was originally produced in 1936, by an anti-marijuana church group hoping to scare kids out of smoking a joint by playing off the stereotypes and falsehoods surrounding cannabis. The original title was *Tell Your Children.* A couple of years later, the famous exploitation film director Dwain Esper acquired it, added more salacious scenes, changed its name to *Reefer Madness,* and screened it across the country for the next decade.

The plot revolves around two evil teenaged dealers, Mae and Jack, who drive poor unsuspecting kids criminally insane by hooking them on marijuana filled cigarettes. A "doctor" tells viewers, "one puff and you're theirs." The heroine of the story is named Mary Lane (no, not Mary Jane) who dies tragically from a stray bullet fired as two pot-crazed kids fight over a loaded gun.

During the 1960s, the acceptance and use of cannabis in mainstream American society grew, while, conversely, its regulation became stricter. President Nixon tightened the screws even further in 1971 by declaring a so-called war on drugs. He said in a speech, "Public enemy number one in the United States is drug abuse. To defeat this enemy, it is necessary to wage a new, all-out offensive."

The real purpose of the war on drugs was motivated by simple politics rather than any public health or law enforcement reason. Top Nixon domestic policy aide John Daniel Ehrlichman, who was convicted for his participation in the Watergate scandal, once explained the Nixon administration's true rationale to a *Harper's* magazine reporter.

"The Nixon campaign in 1968, and the Nixon White House after that, had two enemies: the antiwar left and black people. Understand what I'm saying? We knew we couldn't make it illegal to be either against the war or black, but by getting the public to associate the hippies with marijuana and blacks with heroin, then criminalizing both heavily, we could disrupt those communities. We could arrest their leaders, raid their homes, break up their meetings, and vilify them night after night on the evening news. Did we know we were lying about the drugs? Of course we did," said Ehrlichman. Chilling.

Nixon's efforts worked with ruthless effectiveness—and our criminal justice and prison systems are worse off for it, not to mention society as a whole. In 1970, only 16 percent of the US prison population was behind bars on drug-related offenses. Now, it's a staggering 50.1 percent, per the Federal Bureau of Prisons. The population of federal inmates has meanwhile increased nearly 800 percent since 1980, says the Congressional Research Service. Most astonishingly, marijuana arrests account for over half of all drug arrests in the country, and a clear majority of those are simply for possession, per the American Civil Liberties Union.

The racial numbers are more depressing and alarming. Though usage rates are the same between blacks and whites, African Americans are 3.73 times more likely than whites to be arrested for cannabis. Blacks comprise only 14 percent of the population, yet they're 73 percent of the people incarcerated on drug charges. Additionally, African Americans serve as much time in prison for a drug offense (58.7 months) as whites do for a violent offense (61.7 months), per the Sentencing Project, one of the country's top advocacy groups aimed at reducing incarceration and the burdens placed on the criminal justice system.

President Jimmy Carter took an opposing view to Nixon's upon being elected. In a speech in 1979, he called for the limited decriminalization of cannabis, by allowing people to possess up to one ounce of it. His aim, he said later was "to keep people from being put in prison just because they were smoking a marijuana cigarette." He especially saw the toll the so-called war on drugs took on the black community. Unfortunately, his words fell largely on deaf ears.

In the 1980s, the pendulum swung further toward prohibition, as President Ronald Reagan signed a new law that tightened criminal penalties connected to cannabis even further: possession of one hundred plants earned the same punishment as possession of one hundred grams of heroin. Congress also introduced the "three strikes you're out law," which sent minor repeat drug offenders to jail on life sentences.

All the while, this heavy handed federal approach toward cannabis, and its classification as a Schedule 1 drug, have greatly hurt medical research—to the detriment of humanity. Not that the powerful pharmaceutical lobby minds. That industry revolves around producing more and more specific drugs for different diseases to create a patchwork of cures for each patient. They make more money if someone is on six different prescriptions instead of one holistic solution. A remedy like cannabis, which is naturally produced and keeps the body in balance and promotes homeostasis—can only be a threat.

If cannabis were legalized across the board and people were to reintroduce cannabis oils back into their diets, like in the nineteenth century, Americans would take cannabis-based supplements early in life. The human body, after all, possesses cannabinoid receptors, because there are cannabinoids in breast milk that help babies maintain homeostasis. Cannabis oils promote healthier skin, relieve pain, regulate appetite, alleviate insomnia, and reduce stress, among other benefits.

Dr. Manuel Guzman won the Nobel Prize in Chemistry in 2002 showing that cannabinoids inhibit cancer growth in lab animals and show tremendous potential as a form of treatment for some cancers in humans. Researchers at the University of California San Francisco recently performed four near-identical trials on the effects of cannabis oil on breast cancer. In each case, the test subject was given either a pill or vaporizer. The researchers found that between 77 and 79 percent of patients in stages III or IV of the disease saw a reduction or elimination of the presence of tumors.

Imagine theoretically down the road if a company produces a pill for ten cents a dose that gives people a 77 to 79 percent chance of cancer survival with specific cell types. That's $6 for a two-month supply. Once in remission, someone could take a weekly preventive dose of cannabis oil supplements costing less than $20 a year. Compare those numbers to the cost of chemotherapy, which stretches into the hundreds of thousands of dollars. Cannabis has the potential to revolutionize the cancer industry—for the better for patients, but for the worse for pharmaceutical companies that sell $120 billion worth of cancer drugs globally a year.

No wonder the pharmaceutical industry lobbies aggressively against the end to cannabis prohibition. I am not presenting a conspiracy theory, but a common-sense business strategy, on their part. Other major industries opposed to legalization are alcohol and big tobacco. Just as pharmaceutical firms do not want the curative powers of cannabis to enter the public domain, intoxicant sellers in the US do not want a safe alternative to their products on the market. Since the lifting of the cannabis prohibition in Colorado, for instance, alcohol sales have dropped 10 percent. Did I mention that alcohol and tobacco producers are the primary sponsors of the Partnership for a Drug-Free America?

Another important public health benefit to cannabis legalization would be its effects on the epidemic of addiction to highly destructive drugs. Ending prohibition means people could buy pot at the pot store and not be confronted by someone aggressively trying to push ecstasy, mushrooms, LSD, cocaine, heroin, and the like. Cannabis dispensaries keep consumers in a safe box, protected from crossing over easily into drugs that are not safe for human consumption. A giant first step in tackling America's opioid crisis would be the end of cannabis prohibition.

If you do not believe me, look at Portugal as an example. Portugal, a country of 10.35 million people and a gross national product of $296 billion, took an even more drastic approach to confronting addiction by legalizing all drugs a decade ago. Encouragingly enough, their model has worked without question. In the past decade, hard drug use has dropped by 50 percent, and there is no measured increase of drug consumption of any kind.

Opponents to Portugal's policy initially argued it would unwind civil society and lead to a culture of addiction and abuse. However, the opposite has happened. Unemployment numbers related to drug use have dropped there in the past ten years, as addicts who previously were sent to jail (where they usually have more access to hardcore drugs) are instead sent to treatment centers and returning more productively to their families and workplace. Most importantly, addiction numbers are dropping. If you want to find any negative effects of Portugal's legalization laws, you would need a microscope. Yet, the only way they were passed was through organized and persistent grassroots activism.

A similar groundswell of support for cannabis legalization, at least, has steadily taken root in the US over the past three decades, led largely by the National Organization for the Reform of Marijuana Laws, or NORML. The group formed in the early 1970s not only to support decriminalization, but—through public education—remove the stigma attached to cannabis use. In 1976, NORML gave legal assistance to Robert Randall, a glaucoma sufferer who won a federal court case arguing that smoking cannabis from a plant he was growing on his porch prevented his blindness. This court victory was the first major milestone in the medical marijuana movement. During the following decade, NORML successfully led initiatives to reduce the criminal penalty for marijuana offenses in nearly a dozen states.

In the 1980s, the organization led the charge to provide access to medical marijuana for AIDS sufferers in California—and to alter the public perception on the medicinal benefits of cannabis. The cocktail of drugs created to treat patients suffering from the disease at that time made them as sick as the disease itself, so many turned to cannabis for successful symptom management. Even if laws were not changed overnight, the publicity NORML helped bring to the situation eased enforcement. The San Francisco Police Department began humanely turning a blind eye, for the most part, on black market medicinal cannabis sellers. After all, no one wanted to penalize sick people clinging to life.

A decade later, the citizens of California collectively acted through an election ballot called Proposition 215, also known as the Medical Use of Marijuana Initiative, or the

Compassionate Use Act. Its passage during the 1996 general election gave sick patients the legal right to possess and use—for medical purposes—cannabis to treat a range of ailments, including cancer, anorexia, AIDS, chronic pain, glaucoma, arthritis, migraines, and others.

The law, which passed by a margin of 55.6 percent to 44.4 percent, also protected the doctors who recommended it. The way NORML phrased the issue went something like, "If you oppose this ballot question, you hate cancer patients." For the first time in history, there was a legal construct by a US state that countermanded federal laws on controlled substances.

Proposition 215 was the brainchild of Bay Area activist Dennis Peron, who led the passage of a similar piece of legislation in San Francisco in 1991 (called Proposition P), after watching his longtime partner die of AIDS. A New Yorker profile said Peron challenged "marijuana laws by direct action since 1969 (when he came back from Vietnam with two pounds in his Air Force duffle bag) and by legal and political means since 1970 (when he was first busted)." Near the end of Peron's partner's life in 1990, police entered their house, seized four ounces of pot that his partner was using to ease his AIDS symptoms, and arrested Peron for selling cannabis.

Peron partnered in opening California's first dispensary,

called the San Francisco Cannabis Buyers Club in late 1991. By 1994, it boasted 2,000 members, most of whom were patients with acute illnesses. The business was constantly subjected to legal hassles by federal law enforcement. Officers would arrest him, seize his bank accounts, cash, and cannabis, but never press charges. A few weeks after each ordeal, the Buyers Club would open again, always subject to the possibility that agents would again break down their door.

Leading up to Proposition 215, Peron helped convince the California State legislature to successfully pass statewide medical cannabis legalization laws, but the measures were vetoed by then-governor Pete Wilson. So, Peron—along with other activists and groups like NORML—took the matter directly to the voters in a ballot initiative.

Suddenly, after the 1996 passage of Proposition 215, people could grow a small amount of cannabis, possess it, consume it, and transfer it to other patients (and get reimbursed for their time, effort, and materials) by selling it. The attorney who drafted the language of the initiative was Robert Raich, who became the other godfather of cannabis legalization, alongside Peron. Raich would vigorously defend the legal rights of medical cannabis users for the next two decades.

In the mid-90s, Peron expanded his operation to a five-story building on Market Street in San Francisco. The place was not just a pot bar, but a clubhouse for activists, not to mention a political headquarters, and a therapeutic treatment center. Buds were placed in glass displays and labeled by name, quality, and price. No more than an eighth of an ounce was generally sold. The business also offered edibles and capsules containing cannabinoid oil.

Lines of patients formed around the block every day, but the club maintained impressively strict medical guidelines for customers—though that did not stop several recreational users from successfully making their way through the doors from time to time. The seriously ill customers received their cannabis free of charge. Meanwhile, federal officers continued to raid the club once or twice a year and make a big show of it. Peron was never prosecuted, because even though the boundaries of the law were vague and undefined, he didn't creep outside them.

In 2003, the California legislature enacted Senate Bill 420 to create a more clear-cut (though still imperfect) medical cannabis program. Most notably, it established a voluntary identification card system for patients, and allowed patients to act collectively statewide, like they did on a smaller scale in San Francisco and a handful of other municipalities. Dispensaries sprouted like—for lack of a better term—weeds, and cultivation collectives grew.

The industry expanded so quickly that California legislators and regulators did not know how to respond intelligently. Public policy on cultivation, sales, and possession was piecemeal, always playing catch-up with innovators in the business. The state did not take a regulatory proactive approach until recently with its across-the-board cannabis legalization by following in the footsteps of Colorado and Washington, which both created phenomenal standards for medical and recreational cannabis.

As for the early cannabis grassroots leaders in California: NORML and Raich continue their work, while Peron lives a somewhat quieter life in San Francisco. Raich defended the use of medical cannabis in two cases brought before the US Supreme Court: United States v. Oakland Cannabis Buyers' Cooperative in 2001, and Gonzales v. Raich in 2005. NORML serves an instrumental role in legal cannabis reform through voter initiatives, lobbying on the state and federal level, and providing public education and legal assistance. It boasts more than one hundred chapters across the country.

Today, we have reached a time in American history where the pendulum has rightfully swung fully to the side of cannabis legalization. This is an important moment for the country's public health and justice system—and Colorado and Washington offer a peek into what is in store. In those states, marijuana use among teens has remained the same since recreational legalization, per the *Washington Post*. Marijuana arrests have dropped 50 percent in Colorado, and 98 percent in Washington, the article states. Traffic fatalities remain the same, and tax revenues have risen ($129 million in Colorado and $220 million in Washington). All the while, property crime has fallen by 5 percent, and violent crime has also dropped.

The American cannabis industry has reached an equally pivotal juncture for investors. A breakthrough that transforms the country's economy and way of life only occurs a few times a century. The invention of the cotton gin, the assembly line, and the steam train engine are some examples; the discovery of crude oil and the harnessing of electricity are a few others, along with the creation of the automobile, the invention of the personal computer, and the introduction of the Internet.

Today, a new moment of opportunity has arisen on the edge of cannabis legalization. The fact that there exists a $200 billion industry with not a single company that corners a more measurable slice of market share is mind-boggling. What qualities would enable a company to grab a 1 percent share? How about 5 percent? Or 20 percent? Which investments could potentially lead to a massive profit, and which ones, conversely, to loss and disappointment? These are the questions I aim to answer in greater detail in the coming chapters.

I understand if some potential investors are wary of my vision for the future, and are afraid the federal government will lift the football at the last second, like Lucy with Charlie Brown. There is no way the progress that has been made will be undone, however, and there is no way the legalization's forward momentum can be stopped. There is simply too much public support, and the arguments for legalization's pros—many of which I have mentioned—too greatly exceed the cons.

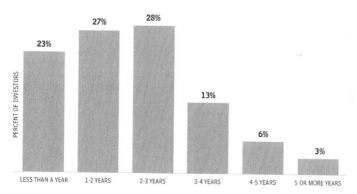

How Long Investors Have Been Funding
Marijuana Businesses

FOUR

An Industry at Work

Centuria Natural Foods is not my first venture on the production side of the cannabis business. I made a damned good crack at it in 2009, with a company called Delta Allied Growers. My intent was to create the first state-approved industrial-scale cannabis nursery in the country, so I exited all positions in retail dispensaries.

While companies like Privateer Holdings spend a lot of money on decades-old techniques that are impossible to scale, I immediately took a different approach and went to Dr. Heiner Lieth, the head of the country's largest plant science department at the University of California, Davis, and hired him as a consultant. He had no experience in growing

cannabis, but was an expert in ornamental horticulture—
the growing of garden plants—on a large industrial scale.
He knew how to grow rows and rows of roses. He knew
how to grow tulips. He knew how to grow strawberries.

Cannabis, after all, is simply another ornamental crop. I
asked him how he would produce it on an industrial level
in a more efficient way than by current methods. He drew
from his experience in the rose and tulip industries to create
a valuable direction strategy for the company. He also told
us that much of the technology used in the strawberry
industry could easily cross over to cannabis cultivation to
improve productivity. Lieth approached cannabis from a
new and innovative direction. Upon his advice, we created
our own specialized nurseries like none ever built before.

Up to that point in early 2009, the largest quasi-legal grower
in the US occupied 40,000 square feet, or about on acre of
space. By contrast, we developed a nursery forty-four times
that size in the small town of Isleton in Sacramento County,
where we intended to become a steady, reliable supplier of
consistent quality goods for medical dispensaries. The local
community was a welcoming and eager partner in the venture, and as part of the arrangement, Delta Allied followed
extremely strict town and state guidelines. Our operation
was wide-open for inspection by local officials and law
enforcement during the construction of our greenhouse

complex, and we were forthcoming and public with our intentions. The concept was revolutionary for its time—in fact, too revolutionary.

Through Leith's assistance, we found and hired one of the country's best plant scientists to boost our operation and became the largest employer in the job-starved region. In May 2011, though, the Department of Justice sent us a letter saying to cease all cannabis operations, or face the possibility of charges being filed against us for violating federal drug laws, "Even if such activities are permitted under state law." My attorney told me I was looking at twenty years to life if prosecuted, even though we were completely law-abiding by California standards.

So, that day, I approached the local police chief and asked him how to properly dispose of our massive inventory of plants. He instructed us to dig a hole and bury it. The county only owned a backhoe that could dig thirteen feet, he said, but a construction excavator could dig as deep as thirty-three. We paid the extra money to rent a local contractor's excavator, dug the three-story-deep hole, dumped all the plants into it, and covered it with dirt.

Our operation at that time was magnitudes larger than any licensed nursery you would find in North America today. Under the law in 2011, patients in the state were each given the right to grow a small amount of marijuana. They could assign those cultivation rights to an outside party or "collective," to produce the plants for them. We worked through dispensaries with large volumes of patients on their rolls to sign up about 60,000 people, whose cultivation rights we legally transferred through dispensary owners. The retailers, in return for working with us, would receive product at a reduced rate. Our business plan fell completely within the parameters of state law, but no one had dared to create a venture so super-sized and ambitious. There was no size limit for producers in our governing municipality, but the ambitious Sacramento County district attorney thought we were too big to ignore, even after we shut our doors. She impaneled a grand jury to investigate—and investigate they did.

To cover our legal bases from the start of the business, we were meticulously diligent with the record keeping; nothing was unaccounted for. We documented every penny spent—and even ones we didn't spend. For instance, if we held a lunch meeting with local officials, we kept our itemized receipts from all meals, showing that the mayor and city council paid their own way (since we were barred by law from picking up their bill).

The grand jury gave all of my employees immunity from prosecution, I guess with the intent of hanging me to dry alone. Bolstering my case was a draft set of cannabis regulations for California, released by state attorney general (and now US Senator) Kamala Harris, which clarified that everything Delta Allied Growers had done to that point was perfectly within state guidelines. Eventually the prosecutor's case fizzled, and the grand jury dissolved after finding no legal violations. No indictments or arrests were handed out. Nothing materialized from it at all but a huge expense to the taxpayers. The whole investigation was simply a circus orchestrated by someone seeking publicity and a future in politics.

ENTER CENTURIA

I have always been emotionally invested in my companies, and the day I received the letter from the prosecutor seemed like the worst single day of my life to that point. Being someone whose first paycheck in the real estate industry after college exceeded the annual amount I expected as a high school teacher following university, I was not used to failure of this kind. By investor estimates, the backhoe buried $72 million in Delta Allied Growers shareholder value. Humbled, disappointed, and left with no other options, I froze the company. I regret I was not able to bring the long-term jobs to Isleton that I and the town officials—who were so accommodating to the venture— were set to produce.

I was back to square one. All the funding I had raised, and all the savings I had invested, were reduced to rubble. I found myself in serious debt to investors—not contractually, but due to an ethical responsibility to honor the first rule of business, "Do what you say you're going to do," and I committed to returning investment to those who trusted me as an operator. After taking about a month to regroup, I realized I needed to brush myself off and move forward. When I was in the retail business, we had suffered setbacks and bounced back, even if the setbacks were not nearly as substantial. I convinced myself I could do it again.

The cannabis industry was so new at that point, I was putting footprints on the moon with every venture I undertook. I learned many fundamental lessons from the Delta Allied Growers experience that have guided me down a more fruitful path ever since. First among them was that patience is not just a virtue in this business, it is required. You cannot push the current of a river to move faster than you would like, no matter how far downstream you can see its course. The flow is too powerful and needs to follow its natural course. The best you can do is position yourself ahead of all others as you ride this current and avoid major obstacles.

I had been so forceful in trying to move the company so rapidly, because I assumed with the Ogden Memo and the aggressive regulations sprouting up in Berkeley and

Oakland, I would have ten well-funded competitors within the year. I left even state officials, like Harris, to play catch-up in deciphering, understanding, and defining the state's regulatory framework. In the process, I left the company exposed to unnecessary obstacles like the ones the prosecutor had arbitrarily built.

Business-wise, I learned if I wanted to expand a company on a high growth trajectory, I could not yet do it domestically, because regulators still were not yet comfortable with permitting mass production facilities—despite the jobs they would create for local economies.

From that moment onward, I laid the groundwork for the creation of Centuria Natural Foods. I knew the company had to be internationally licensed and permitted; nimble enough to expand quickly as barriers to cannabis sales and consumption inevitably tumbled; large enough to create economies of scale; technologically advanced enough to shatter the paradigm on old production methods; and patient enough to wait for proper regulatory structures in Canada and the US to be set in place.

In terms of paradigm-shattering innovation, Centuria's breakthrough business model starts with our proprietary propagation system. Though virtually all cannabis nurseries hand clone, this method is simply too labor intensive to mimic on a mass scale, of say, a thousand-ton production run. So, instead, we use a unique system we have developed ourselves.

In it, our plantings are layered in phases to create a continual process within the seasonal window of harvesting. Generally, the time from dropping the plantlets into the ground until harvesting is 110 days. The process of drying, extraction of ingredients, and manufacturing and packaging takes about another one hundred days. In other words, we can go from propagation to shelf in 210 days—which, given how efficiently we work, is about the same turnaround time as an old-fashioned hand-propagating nursery, yet at a fraction of the cost and more importantly, a fraction of the resources. Competitive turnaround times are essential in the global market, no matter what the scale of the company, to maximize use of space, meet changing demands, and keep prices low.

Even though I have partially revealed what our cultivating process is, I have not said exactly how we do it. It has been developed over a decade in the laboratory. Our investment in identifying new plant varieties alone is difficult to match, let alone our equipment and techniques for growing them. Investing in simply keeping our breeding program operational, along with supplying the necessary facilities, has cost millions, for example.

We also must set aside a certain amount of square footage of valuable canopy space for research and development—a resource most other producers cannot match. In places like Colorado, Washington, and California, manufacturers are extremely limited in canopy size by regulation and do not have the luxury of dedicating a single square inch of it to anything but growing plants for commercial use. For that reason, they are better off simply hand-cloning or hand-propagating, then moving on to the next new and popular varietal a couple of years later when it arises. They do not have the ability or patience to spend two years on R&D the way we do.

Of course, the hand propagation methods the smaller nurseries use do give them an advantage in keeping quicker pace with changing consumer trends—but we more than offset this situation by producing equal quality products at drastically lower prices. Whenever Centuria enters a new market with an offering 80 percent cheaper than what a small nursery is selling, buyers will think primarily with their wallets.

In that way, the cannabis business is like the wine business. With wine, there are connoisseurs willing to spend $700 on a bottle of Chateau Lafite or even more on Shafer Sunspot, but they do not drink it every night. Instead, they spend that kind of money maybe only a few of times a year. What they normally put on their table for dinner each night costs probably $15 to $50 a bottle. We are equal in every way to that $15 to $50 bottle, except our offering sells for a fraction of that price.

I have learned in the cannabis industry that the R&D process can never stop, because tastes and trends change. To use another analogy, think of cannabis like another ornamental crop: tomatoes. There was a time when consumers were happy with a few different generic varietals like beefsteak, plum, and cherry. Then, some amazing and unique heirloom varieties appeared, and tastes changed. Now, every season, new and different heirlooms hit the vegetable stands (and even supermarkets), and customer palates—and demands—noticeably shift. In addition, preferences differ from region to region, and even city to city.

Today in cannabis, there are two North American epicenters of innovation, both on the West Coast: Southern California, and the Emerald Triangle around Humboldt County in the northern part of the Golden State. They each cater to two different tastes. Southern California's market appeals to a higher priced retail market. Consumers demand a higher aesthetic—it needs to look better—and will pay 20 to 30 percent higher prices than in Colorado, Washington, and Northern California. They are looking for the multi-colored, interesting looking heirloom tomatoes.

The Emerald Triangle's local retail market is more budget-based and consumers are more concerned with price than aesthetics. They are attracted to creative twists on slightly more conventional strains. While varietals developed in one of these areas eventually does seep into the other market, it takes a couple of years to occur.

Most other industries—whether it is biotech, agriculture, medicine, academia, or whatever—collectively hold conferences and publish industry research journals to share ideas and celebrate breakthroughs. Innovators in these fields are writing papers and giving lectures on their research and discoveries, and advances are often open-source to promote the free trade of ideas and create a better world. You go to a cannabis trade show today, however, and producers are hoarding information like they are clutching onto their last can of soup in a fallout shelter after the apocalypse.

This is obviously not my philosophy—and I think the lack of transparency will be the demise of the cottage cannabis grower. Like I mentioned earlier in the book, without pooling information and efforts in a cooperative manner, they will not have the resources to compete with the market behemoths. The price of labor, land, processing, and manufacturing will become too steep for the cottage industry. If cultivators operate cooperatively, though, they could share costs for fertilizer, and substrate. They could collectively invest in infrastructure and equipment that brings down their manufacturing costs. A single grower might not be able to afford a single high-end piece of machinery, but fifty growers in an area could, and if they share it, they can all reduce expenses and potentially thrive.

Across the board, all industry players will be forced into sharing everything from growing techniques to genetic material, out of necessity—no differently than they do in other agricultural segments. If I was a corn grower today, for instance, I would pay dues to the National Corn Growers Association, and they in turn would give me annual data on the research they conduct on all sorts of variables—from which variety of corn grows best in my environment to what the optimal growing conditions are to maximize those yields. Everything is shared, and they have more than 40,000 dues-paying members. They even share seeds—ones you cannot get in a Burpee packet in the hardware store. There is no similar cannabis growers association.

The closest cannabis cultivation has to an industry conference is the Emerald Cup. Founded in 2003, and hosted in Sonoma County in California, it is the Super Bowl of cannabis growers. Most high-market-value new varietals developed by growers are showcased here. More than 10,000 people attend annually, and the highlight is the competition for the Cup itself, bestowed upon what is judged to be the best cannabis strain of the year. Last year, more than 900 entries were registered—and each was graded on its smell, taste, looks, vibrancy and effects (or "how it changes the consciousness"). Every product is required to be organic and sun-grown.

Creating a new varietal for the Emerald Cup is as much an art as it is a science. A shift in strains can be incredibly small and still make a remarkable difference in final product—since cannabis is grown for both its psychoactive and aromatic qualities. Consider that there are roughly 500 cannabinoids (the primary psychoactive compound) and terpenes (the fragrant oils that provide flavor) combined in a plant. Each new combination of these ingredients creates a unique effect and carves out its own spot for the strain in the marketplace.

The winning Emerald Cup entry automatically fetches a high consumer price, and the creator guards the molecular makeup the way Coca Cola guards its secret formula. The strain itself, though, is only part of the story. Cultivation techniques are equally as important in creating a quality end-product. You can give the same varietal to twenty different growers, and you will end up with twenty different results, as they all cultivate in varying ways.

Yet, none of these products will hit the market on a mass

scale anytime soon, because there is no massive seed bank promoted by the industry that brings the seeds to growers, and no one shares their secrets. Instead, the market is filled with boutique players who make what equates to their own proprietary craft batches. Since no one will play together nicely, and there is no collectively funded breeding program to create a ready supply of ultra-stable genetic stock—like with corn, soy, and wheat—the horizon is empty of promise.

In ancient Greek tragedies, it is always hubris—or excessive and foolish pride—that leads to the hero's downfall. Hubris leads most cottage industry players over the cliff. There is still time for attitudes to change in this segment of the business, and for cooperation to be effective and profitable, but not much.

When I refer to genetics, it is important for me to note I focus on hybrids and not genetic modification. Hybrid seeds are created by the cross pollination of seed varieties, usually—but not always—in a controlled environment. Hybrid seeds have been used for generations to create hardier crops that are more resistant to drought, disease, and pests, and will produce higher yields. They can also create more visually desirable crops. Genetic modification, on the other hand, is the process of creating a new plant by combining the DNA of two species that couldn't cross-breed naturally. For instance, when scientists weave together the genetic material of corn with that of a bacterium that will kill pests that try to eat it.

The original, landrace forms of cannabis, as it grew in the wild, is naturally an extremely vigorous plant that thrives in a wide range of weather conditions and is highly pest resistant. It truly is an amazing plant. The cannabis grown commercially in the US, though, is nothing like it. Over the generations, cultivators have manipulated the genetics through hybrid breeding techniques to produce more appealing aromatic and psychoactive traits. The product that is available today, for instance, produces significantly more tetrahydrocannabinol (or as it is commonly known, THC) than the cannabis on the market just a decade ago.

Take the popular cannabis strain called Haze as an example. It was created in Northern California in the late 1960s by Sam the Skunkman, Wernard, Neville, and Eddie Reedeker, as a hybrid from domesticated seed-grown plants from Mexico, Colombia, and the Far East. Since that time, it has served as the evolutionary building block for several Cannabis Cup winning strains. Yet, today's versions are exponentially more psychoactive than anything produced fifty years ago. In all, it is safe to say cannabis is the most hybridized, over-bred crop in human history besides corn.

I have found that cannabis consumers do not generally

mind hybridization, but they do adamantly demand a pesticide and solvent-free product that is not genetically modified. Some buyers will ask for a certificate of analysis produced by an outside laboratory proving the plants are raised, harvested, and processed naturally. By contrast, you do not see people walking into their local Trader Joe's and asking for proof of the same high standards on the organic tomatoes or spinach they buy. Producers will need to realize that as they expand, they cannot simply add more chemicals or genetically splice their way to a higher output. Their customers won't stand for it.

For that reason, Centuria relies on the polyculture method of farming instead of monocropping. Monocropping, or monoculture, is what you see in the rows of crops grown in the Midwest. Drive down the interstate between the Mississippi and the Rockies, and you are bound to be surrounded by tens of thousands of acres of one crop, like corn, wheat, or soy, stretching into the rural horizon. That single crop is planted on the same plot of land every year, without fail. The farmers use special pesticides, herbicides, and other chemicals to eliminate any other organism in that environment except for the one they are growing. They do not want any natural enemies or competition for those plants.

Monocropping farmers face a constant battle, though,

because nature always finds a way to cancel out human efforts to control or conquer it. New pests will move in with old ones gone, and new diseases will arise in wake of the absence of others. The gaps are inevitably filled. As Michael Pollan wrote in *The Omnivore's Dilemma*: "Mother Nature destroys monocultures." Think of the millions of gallons of chemicals needed in the monocrop approach, all of which eventually leeches into the water supply. Not to mention the devastation to the topsoil.

With the polyculture model, farmers rotate crops to maintain a more natural balance—and introduce beneficial microorganisms and insects. In Centuria's case, we use winter cover crops. If we grow cannabis during the summer, we cultivate a different plant in the cold-weather months that rejuvenates the soil and ecosystem, and does not fight for the same resources. This strategy reduces our use of chemicals, or the need for genetically modified plants. In the coming decade, consumers will demand this type of growing approach.

Portion Of Wholesale Cultivators Using Chemicals For Pests, Molds, Fungi Or Mildew

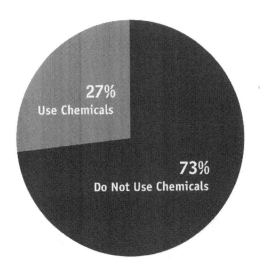

27%
Use Chemicals

73%
Do Not Use Chemicals

How Do Wholesale Cultivators That Do Not Use Chemicals Prevent Pests, Molds, Fungi Or Mildew?

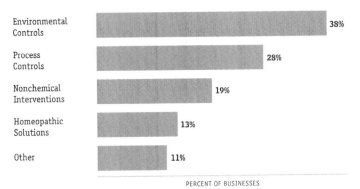

Environmental Controls	38%
Process Controls	28%
Nonchemical Interventions	19%
Homeopathic Solutions	13%
Other	11%

PERCENT OF BUSINESSES

FIVE

Broadening the Scope

The prime example of an organically minded outdoor nursery in the US is Los Sueños Farm in Colorado. They use native insects to control pests without pesticides and in 2016, they harvested 21,600 plants of fifty-five different strains on their thirty-six acres, per media accounts. They employ eighty workers, making them one of the most efficient large-scale nurseries on the continent. Excluding the three-quarters of an acre they allocate to greenhouse space, they operate seasonally, with plants placed in the ground in April, and harvested in October or November. They are one of the few cannabis companies in the US, I should point out, to use tractors at any stage of production.

By contrast, consider an anonymously named cultivation site *Farm X*, which is one of the largest *indoor* nurseries in Colorado. They operate like a traditional warehouse nursery with maybe one hundred people working different parts of the building, which occupies two acres of land. This is the type of setup repeated by hundreds of cannabis producers in the US and Canada. They are not working seasonally and are instead producing twenty-four hours a day, seven days a week, twelve months a year, with grow-lights burning, sprinklers misting, and farm hands meticulously tending.

They are a profitable operation today, but they lack the ability to scale, given that they spent $4 million an acre developing their site, not to mention the overhead. If they produce, for the sake of argument, five tons a year at a cost of $2 a gram, this is an unsustainable cost when you compete against a company manufacturing a comparable product for a nickel a gram. There is also a ceiling, so to speak, over their business, because they only grow indoors. There is only so much warehouse or greenhouse space a producer can occupy before the real estate, construction, electricity, and maintenance costs become too prohibitive.

In every US state that allows cannabis cultivation, growing permits are limited in terms of canopy space. This is the amount of area, in square feet, measured around the tops of the plants being grown. If a state grants you a half-acre of canopy space, you are naturally going to dedicate every square inch to cultivating biomass. You will not want any walking space.

This is the only measurement that seems to work. Plant count is not an effective parameter for regulators, because the size, thickness, and height of plants can vary so greatly—and be manipulated. Regulating the size of an operation's footprint does not work either, because some manufacturers build growing facilities several stories tall and use vertical farming techniques. I think vertical farming is a promising approach, but there is no incentive, based on the canopy size rules, to innovate with it at this time.

Instead, every US nursery is intent on maximizing the number of grams of product they can churn out per square foot of canopy, and they obsess over business growth within those narrow boundaries. Regulators have been effective in promoting this mindset, and because the market has been profitable to this point for producers, no one has needed to think outside this literal and figurative box. For producers to make profits going forward, they will need to burn this box to the ground. Centuria will force them to do it, because our growing techniques, mass production capabilities, and breakthrough business model will leave them no choice.

We will force more producers into the sunlight. Until now, most legal nurseries—besides Los Sueños and a few others— use only indoor cultivation facilities, like *Farm X*. They are under the misguided impression that the only way to grow great cannabis is by completely controlling the environment, and of course high quality is essential. Just as discerning diamond buyers look for the "four Cs" (color, clarity, cut, and carat weight) when making purchasing decisions, discerning cannabis buyers also use four metrics for measuring value: aromatics, potency, trichome structures (the hair-like crystals on the bud), and bud density. Producers do not want to add the wild card of nature into the equation of perfecting a plant, for fear of losing precise control over these distinctive and fickle measurements.

Yet, natural sunlight generates 40 percent more photosynthetic activity than the most advanced artificial light in the world. This, therefore, generates more biomass, in the way nature intended. Centuria shows how to strike success outdoors and in greenhouses while still maintaining the "four Cs." We do it by borrowing strategies employed by successful growers of other plant types, and re-engineering them to fit our business. Along the way, we drastically reduce labor costs. Compared to indoor nurseries, which employ 135 people per acre, we employ less than two.

The actual (and more importantly, perceived) risk of working in the legal cannabis industry has become so low that you can recruit highly paid professionals from other industries to work in it now. A decade ago, if I approached the CEO of a billion-dollar company and asked him to work for a company like Centuria, he would have told me to get lost. Today, executives and scientists understand the federal government's stance on the issue, and recognize the opportunity that the new green rush presents. Many want to jump from their high-paying jobs with established corporations to test the cannabis field, to the benefit of well-funded operations like Centuria. I can say with great pride that this path has allowed me to work with some of the most brilliant scientists in the world.

When Centuria confronts an "impossible" problem—whether it is biological, chemical, or mechanical—we identify a specific person with the background and ability to solve it, no matter what industry they are in, and then recruit them to work with us, either on a long- or short-term basis. I will often personally knock on a person's door, at their home or office, to make the pitch to both the potential hire, but more importantly, their significant other (a recruitment tool employed by my father). Many are surprisingly eager at the right opportunity to become a trailblazer in the cannabis field.

In the past, specialists from other fields decidedly did not want their collaboration with us to be made public—especially those who worked in academia. They were afraid of being blackballed by their peers at best, or getting fired or losing their tenure as university professors and researchers at worst. This attitude has vanished recently, though, and opened the doors of opportunity for Centuria.

The massive cultural shift toward cannabis acceptance cannot be credited to one moment in time or milestone—not even the passage of recreational laws in Washington, Colorado, or California, or the efforts of NORML. It cannot be attributed to one ballot initiative, or federal pronouncement, either. It was more organic, and it incorporated these factors—mixed with the collective common sense of the American public. The cultural shift was a tectonic movement, led by legions of activists across the country until people in places of power began catching up to mass consensus on legalization.

Millennials especially recognize the way the playing field is artificially tilted against cannabis—and they rapidly overshadow Baby Boomers in electoral power. They understand the hypocrisy behind the federal government classifying cannabis as a Schedule I drug, yet holding the patent on its medical use. They also understand the hypocrisy of that small, dwindling number of Baby Boomers (who came of age in a haze of pot smoke, themselves) trying to place their thumbs on the wrong end of the scale of justice. There is only one direction for the tectonics to continue to move: toward progress.

Typical Wholesale Cultivator Annual Operating Costs Per Square Foot By Cultivation Type

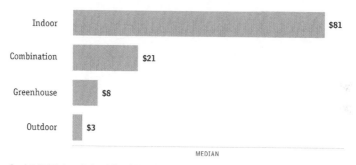

Indoor	$81
Combination	$21
Greenhouse	$8
Outdoor	$3

MEDIAN

SIX

Winning the future

Thomas Edison said, "I have not failed, I've just found 10,000 ways that won't work." When Delta Allied Growers closed its doors, I first considered the venture a failure. Those experiences, though, enabled me to position Centuria for the growth and success it enjoys today. It was my investors who persuaded me to pull the plug on Allied. They were smart, accomplished, business-savvy people who understood the threat the letter from federal prosecutors posed. Even if the company was eventually vindicated in the courts, the battle would have been long and costly. It was time to cut bait, they told me. My investors are the types who expect eight out of ten of their startup investments to go belly-up as two go to the moon. In their eyes,

Delta Allied was one of the eight, and they were okay with it.

Any sane person would have thrown in the towel at that moment, yet I still wanted to reward those investors for their faith. To use another quote from a famous dead guy, Winston Churchill once declared, "Success is not final, failure is not fatal: it is the courage to continue that counts."

I do not know if it was courage that motivated me to continue, but grit and tenacity surely factored into the equation. Plus, if my options were either to take a mid-level manager's job at a buddy's company, or try to shoot the moon to lead the first private billion-dollar company in the cannabis industry, I knew which path to choose.

Delta Allied was a hundred times larger in scale than any licensed cannabis company in the world when it closed. We had developed the foundational technology, and I knew the mathematics behind the model was sound. The problem with Delta Allied was that it was based on the economics of where the cannabis industry would be in 2019, not where it was in 2009. The notion still applied that only manufacturers capable of scaling their operations rapidly would someday corner the cannabis market. Unfortunately, though, a clearly defined legal framework had not yet been settled upon to protect large producers.

Thus, I basically told the investors, "Guys, the journey is not going to end here. I'm never going to stop until this venture succeeds. I'll make sure you get your investment back, with interest." By the time you're finished reading this book, my debts, with interest, have been paid.

This is what allowed me to continue research towards my original goal of further developing the technology to change a global industry. I realized to legally grow cannabis on an industrial scale, I needed to look beyond America's borders—at least until federal attitudes changed and state laws became more defined. I, therefore, turned my attention to Latin America and worked with a pharmaceutical consultant who had made inroads with the ministers of health of nearly all the countries in the region with companies such as British Zenica. He convinced the government of El Salvador, along with the country's highest medical research hospital, to grant Centuria's predecessor permission to research cannabinoid-class drugs in that country.

Most Latin American countries share enlightened views on cannabis consumption, and they are eager to lure businesses within their borders. El Salvador, for instance, offers a ten-year tax holiday for foreign companies working there, and was enthusiastic to partner with the company. As part of the arrangement, the health minister asked for full transparency and complete access to all our records. He also needed assurances that law enforcement officers from his office could pay our facilities random visits whenever they wanted. Done deal.

Centuria's predecessor also was not allowed to cultivate cannabis in El Salvador, which—looking back now—is probably a good thing for my health, and that of the people who work for my company. The country suffers from the second-highest murder rate, per capita, in the world, and its organized crime networks are among the most ruthless and sophisticated anywhere. Two major gangs in El Salvador extort money from roughly 40 percent of the legal businesses there. When their payments aren't received, they kill or kidnap to get their money. The gangs probably would not have taken kindly to a legal cannabis grower whose business threatened their own black market production.

Being based in that country, though, and having a government-approved research permit, gave us legitimacy—and a foothold—with El Salvador's neighboring countries, where we also opened a new base of operations. Our scientific research in these places enabled us to find a way to separate the THC molecules in a cannabis plant from the CBD in 2014. This was a huge breakthrough.

Put simply, THC is the psychoactive cannabinoid that provides the "high." CBD, on the other hand (or cannabidiol), provides many of marijuana's medical and therapeutic benefits. CBD-only products hit the US market in 2010, and by 2014, their acceptance—because they're non-psychoactive—across the country grew. Today, they are legal in forty-four states.

Centuria is the only company in the US that can separate THC and CBD on an industrial scale, allowing us to produce CBD-only products better, faster, and cheaper than anyone else in the world. After 2013, we moved our production and research facilities to Europe—first to Spain and then the Czech Republic. As successful as our efforts in Central America were, the culture of corruption among the bureaucracy in some countries there stretched beyond our level of comfort.

By 2015, we continued our research while exporting CBD-only biomass from Europe into the US, and manufacturing cannabis oil products on a large scale domestically. I should note, though, the goal of the company is not to be an industrial hemp oil supplier. Centuria's aim is to create manufacturing systems that can mass-produce consumables containing all cannabinoids, including THC, or supply ingredients for other product manufacturers. CBD-only products opened more doors for us, and allowed Centuria to test practices and production methods on a larger scale than ones containing THC did.

I believe the fastest growing segment of the cannabis space soon will be low-THC products. By possessing a higher ratio of cannabinoids that produce lower narcotic effects, they offer a very different user experience. There are many people who are no longer interested in high-THC products but still want to enjoy the aromatic, aesthetic, or—more importantly—therapeutic qualities of other cannabinoids. In other words, they want the benefits of cannabis, but don't necessarily want to get stoned.

This kind of product is bound to experience the largest market capture in the coming years, because it occupies a new and virtually untapped segment. I foresee a time in the not-too-distant future when low or no-THC cannabis products sit on the supermarket, drug store, and department store shelves beside the likes of Tums and Advil.

With the advantage of hindsight, my tenacity after the Delta Allied Growers experience truly was a virtue. My friends and family might call my single-mindedness a flaw sometimes, other times a mental disorder. But there is something to be said for not giving up on an idea that you know will work. I remember my father pleading with me in 2014, "Michael please, just take a job with one of your friends. Come back to the cannabis industry in a year or two, but take a break."

I could not take a break, though. Centuria's research and

development teams made constant breakthroughs—and even though R&D can be crippling financially, the strides we made were too important to simply put on a shelf. One breakthrough was our creation of a bench-scale model of an oil extraction device that could operate with 96 percent efficiency of molecular capture. Creating a larger version capable of producing a ton of oil a day was exceedingly expensive—and risky if it did not work. Every prototype failure meant millions of dollars (literally vapor) going up in smoke—and we suffered three or four of these setbacks a year, every year.

Yet, we used each trip back to drawing board as a learning experience, and a chance to examine exactly what went wrong, and what worked, with our approach. All the while, we continued to climb the slow ladder of progress. In 2016, for instance, we conducted a massive equipment overhaul that increased our production capacity by 3,000 percent but required us to shut down our facilities for almost six months.

The entire system was supposed to be implemented in mid-June of that year, but the equipment delivery was delayed, and it did not go online until late July. Three weeks later, a specialized, custom-made piece of machinery meant to last for years broke in a matter of weeks—sending us offline again. Inventing and producing a more reliable replacement took another five weeks. So, during those months, we had minimal manufacturing capacity. The burn rate was reduced to a manageable level, but every penny of burn was necessary to increase our capacity exponentially. These types of experiences happen every year, while at the same time, our production capacity has grown by an average of 1,000 percent annually for almost three years. Bringing big ideas to life isn't for the faint of heart.

BURSTING THE BUBBLE

I am the most optimistic person you will ever meet—regardless of the situation. Even when Delta Allied Growers shut down, or when we hit hiccups like in 2016 at Centuria, I looked at the silver lining of the situation, probably to a fault. This mindset of mine is a huge asset when everything looks like it is going wrong, though, because I concentrate on finding the solution, always convinced it is somewhere within reach if I just look hard enough for it. Equally important were the people who unwaveringly supported me through these failures.

I do not know if my optimism is infectious, but at the least it is moderately contagious with my team. When the people around me thought of throwing in the towel during some challenging time, I told them, "Hold on. Here's why this is the eve before our greatest triumph." They have faith in my track record, and in my level of complete commitment to our company's mission. I would be remiss to point out that I rely on them more than the other way around.

My team believes deeply in Centuria's breakthrough business plan and strategy. Our company has built a solid foundation atop the world's most advanced methods for the mass production of high quality, low cost cannabis products. We show direct, tangible results, and not simply making vague promises on future performance. I like to contrast our approach to that of the Canadian company Canopy Growth Partners, which takes advantage of an investment bubble in cannabis that is bound to burst.

Canopy Growth is, as they say, all sizzle and no steak. They sell an archaic strategy and market the hell out of it. The company made some great headlines when they went public on the Toronto Stock Exchange under the symbol WEED in 2016, for instance. They also have a partnership deal with Snoop Dogg. Their headquarters occupies a historic Hershey chocolate factory near Niagara Falls and includes 350,000 square feet of attractive greenhouse space. Flush with investor dollars, they aggressively bought competitors. Canopy Growth will be the first to tell you that they are run by Harvard MBAs and Cambridge law graduates, but their production model at $3.03 per gram per their latest quarterly report is, frankly, dumb.

Stripped down to the basics, they are a billion-dollar company that is only producing $27 million in revenue right now. Canopy Growth sells investors on its rapid growth, which is only coming from buying other companies for too much money and absorbing their revenue—not by increasing their own sales. They boast that they can potentially bring in hundreds of millions of dollars in revenue, but their projection is based on producing cannabis at over $3 a gram, which is exponentially higher than the pennies per gram that Centuria already achieved in 2016. Besides the sleek marketing, they offer nothing extraordinary to the consumer—not unique quality or price—that will create a mass exodus of consumers to drop other brands and come to them.

How massive is the investment bubble around Canopy Growth? Consider that the price to earnings ratio of its stock is around an 86. Meanwhile, Facebook's is 33, Apple's is 16, and Reynolds American's is roughly 13. When Centuria and Canopy Growth compete in any federalized market, the bubble will burst, because Canopy's business model will not function. Their production methods are simply way too costly, and their value as a company will be little more than whatever the real estate of the old Hershey factory is worth. Companies like Tilray, which I mentioned earlier in the book, will be worse off. They spent $40 million an acre on a factory that produces cannabis for over $3 a gram—in comparison with our $28,000 an acre and less than five cents a gram.

Marijuana Stock Gains In 2016 Versus S&P 500

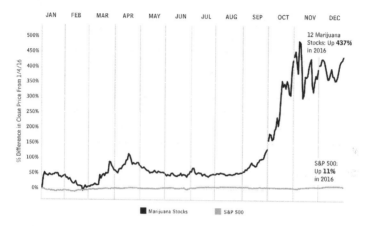

Conclusion

———

In 1755, the father of economics, Adam Smith, first wrote about the "invisible hand" of the free market economy. The basic philosophy was that when the government gets out of the business of regulating a commodity, its supply and demand (and price) will be dictated almost exclusively by the market. Producers will want to make as much profit as possible, while consumers will want to pay the lowest prices they can for a quality product. So, if an entrepreneur can find a profitable way to charge less money for a well-crafted item than his or her competitors, consumers will quickly flock to him or her.

Smith knew the best way to appeal to the public is through their own self-interest—which means the product you sell must present the greatest perceived value to consumers for them to buy it. Most high-profile cannabis ventures have completely forgotten this simple notion. Investor darlings like Tilray and Canopy Growth are so intently focused on profit, given the industry's multi-billion-dollar potential, that they ignore perceived value. They generate products that are of no better price or quality than what's already available on the market—because they use the same old production methods as everyone else. They do not present a better buy for consumers, only better marketing. Savvy people are only mildly swayed by flashy packaging and Snoop Dogg endorsements, though. Instead, they are more motivated by their own self-interest and have no reason to switch brands to Tilray and Canopy Growth.

From the start, Centuria's intent has been to find the best balance between quality, profitability, and undeniable value—and we have achieved it. Just as important, even though we are likely the world's largest cannabis man-ufacturer by gross tonnage, we know how to affordably expand our operations by factors of ten to meet immense demand when the US and Canadian market barriers are lifted, and the invisible hand of the free market pushes cannabis consumers in our direction. If it is not, for some reason, Centuria that lures customers away from the Tilrays and Canopy Growths of the world, it will be some other entity competing alongside us that also boasts a more effi-cient way of doing business.

Entrepreneurs and investors in the cannabis industry are naturally resistant to overturn the old cultivation and production methods because taking risk is difficult, and uncomfortable—and human beings don't like being uncomfortable. That has not been our problem at Centuria. Every step of our process is conducted in a way that has never been done before—like shifting from the controlled environment of a warehouse nursery through proprietary cultivation technologies; merging cannabis farming techniques with those used in modern agricultural systems; and the simple use of sustainable farming practices.

There were years when Centuria experienced 70 to 90 percent molecular losses with R&D from testing new approaches and technologies, and that is a terrible position to be in. It can be disheartening. However, each failure has set us further down the path toward success. They have led us to better understand what works, or as Edison said, what does not work. The setbacks we have experienced would break most people's morale, but we at Centuria have kept marching forward. This persistence has paid off, and is what has allowed us to find ourselves in the commanding position we do today.

The risk-averse, old-school approach to cannabis production won't stop the invisible hand of the free markets from sweeping aside the people and companies stuck in a stagnant mindset. I look forward to seeing the other ventures that someday develop revolutionary methods to provide high quality products at significantly lower prices. All of this will come once the artificial barriers to entry—such as current federal regulations—are removed for cannabis. If we produce cannabis at $1.26 an ounce in 2016, the wholesale cost will move to within 10 to 20 percent of that number, and the Tilrays and Canopy Growths of the world will collapse.

Brand identity cannot save the old producers, either. My experience has shown me there is little loyalty among cannabis consumers. I discovered early in my career in California that when one dispensary undercut the prices of another down the street, customers left the higher-priced one in droves. I employed this pricing strategy a handful of times, by selling eighth-ounces of legal medical marijuana for $5 to $15 cheaper than at nearby dispensaries. These competitors cut their labor force within a few months by 65 percent, because their patient count has dropped by more than that.

Cannabis consumers are among the most sophisticated buyers in any market. They spend a huge percentage of their income on it—no different from wine or Scotch lovers who spend on their drink of choice—so they keep extremely well-informed on what they purchase. They are attuned to the ever-changing market value of cannabis, and once they find quality at a cheaper price, they never go back to a retailer or brand that is unwilling or unable to maintain competitive pricing. They are too attuned to make that mistake.

The big question, of course, is knowing when the free markets will truly prevail, and the cannabis prohibition finally ends in the US. Fortunately, Colorado and Washington have created an exemplary roadmap for the deregulation of adult-use of recreational cannabis. Many other states will roll out legalization in similar ways, and success will beget more success. Legislators on the state and national levels can only ignore the overwhelming will of the people for so long, especially as cannabis consumption is repeatedly shown to be safe and, at times, beneficial across the country. By the early 2020s, for every one voter who is against legalization across the country, two voters will support it.

Like in Colorado and Washington, legalization in most states will (and should) include strong consumer protection laws requiring third-party testing to ensure there are no harmful additives in the products, and there will be limits on the size of nurseries within the US, because they will be easier to manage and inspect. This cautious approach will be a hindrance to nurseries based domestically who want to compete on a global scale. In Centuria's case, with large internationally based nurseries, we stand only to gain from this situation and the limits placed on our domestic competitors.

Given the trajectory of legalization, the legalization of interstate cannabis commerce will likely occur within five years. This will tear down a titanic artificial barrier to free market forces. The most efficient farms in states like California, Washington, and Colorado will enter other state markets to reach a broader consumer base and make more profit, for instance. Costs will instantly go down because of the increased competition, and quality will improve. Consumers, acting in their own self-interest by looking for the best product at the best price, will force the market to meet their demand.

In the long-term future, as the market expands, the average consumer will gravitate toward cannabis as a safer alternative to tobacco and alcohol as an intoxicant. We have already seen a potential shift in this direction in Colorado, where alcohol consumption rates have slightly decreased since cannabis prohibition ended.

From a public health standpoint, this would be a positive trend. Cannabis is infinitely safer than alcohol—considering that there has never been a single recorded example of a fatal pot overdose. Meanwhile, by contrast, I can walk into a liquor store right now and easily buy enough alcohol to kill myself without the sales clerk batting an eye. Of course, one of the single biggest killers in the country is tobacco. Lung cancer accounts for about 27 percent of cancer deaths, taking the lives of roughly 160,000 American men and women annually.

By contrast, studies of links between regular marijuana smokers and cancer show a minuscule cause and effect, at best. In fact, a UCLA pulmonologist, who researched cannabis for three decades, conducted a study involving 1,200 people that showed no connection whatsoever between smoking marijuana and cancer. Funded in part by the National Institutes of Health, the study was the largest of its kind ever conducted. More research on the subject obviously needs to be done, but because cannabis is classified as a Schedule 1 drug, researchers are limited in what they're allowed to do.

Another reality legislators ultimately cannot ignore is the fact marijuana is the largest revenue-producing crop in every single US state. It is produced and sold everywhere, but not taxed in states where prohibition still exists, because transactions are made in the black market. Simply placing a 3 percent tax on cannabis would be a boon for any state. Colorado, for instance, uses its cannabis revenue to provide college grants. Under this model, kids, parents, and schools win.

A substantial percentage of investors today are concerned about federal law enforcement. People with assets in many places can be reluctant to invest in something the US government hasn't formally legalized. No one wants to go to jail for investing in cannabis, myself among them. I appreciate this concern—even if it is largely unfounded, since the federal government has been clear on its enforcement policies in states where cannabis is legal.

Stay standing on the sidelines if you do not feel comfortable right now, but be warned that as the industry becomes more normalized in the eyes of investors, you do so at your peril. Capital already moves more freely to the cannabis space, as the number of investment funds dedicated to raising and deploying assets within it is rapidly expanding. This improving environment will further enable efficient companies with breakthrough business models like Centuria's to thrive and seize massive slices of market share. Yes, these truly are high times in the cannabis business.

Top Mistakes Private Cannabis Businesses Make When Seeking Funding, According To Investors

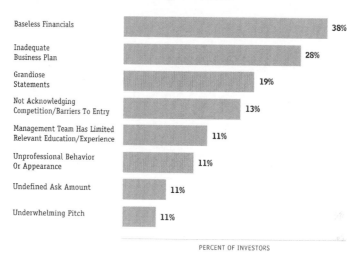

Baseless Financials	38%
Inadequate Business Plan	28%
Grandiose Statements	19%
Not Acknowledging Competition/Barriers To Entry	13%
Management Team Has Limited Relevant Education/Experience	11%
Unprofessional Behavior Or Appearance	11%
Undefined Ask Amount	11%
Underwhelming Pitch	11%

PERCENT OF INVESTORS

Note: Multiple-choice question, respondent total may be greater than 100%.

Copyright 2017 Marijuana Business Daily, a division of Anne Holland Ventures Inc. All rights reserved.

About the Author

MICHAEL BRUBECK is an entrepreneur and financial specialist who has spent nearly two decades building businesses in the pharmaceutical research and the legal cannabis industries. He's the CEO of Centuria Natural Foods, the largest cannabis manufacturer by gross tonnage in North America. Brubeck currently resides in Dallas.

Made in the USA
Lexington, KY
30 October 2017